The
Simple Bites
Kitchen

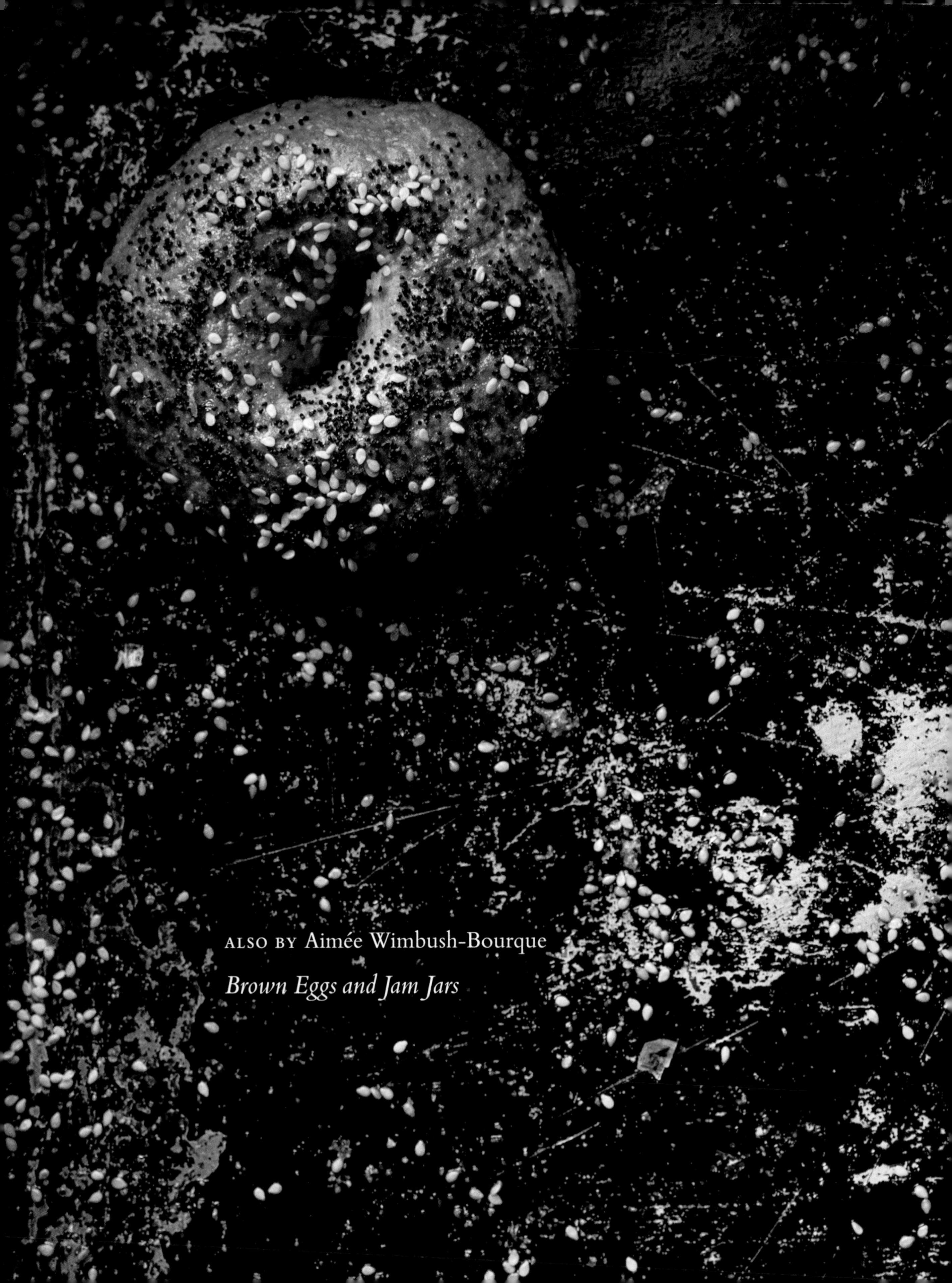

ALSO BY Aimée Wimbush-Bourque

Brown Eggs and Jam Jars

The
Simple Bites
Kitchen

NOURISHING WHOLE FOOD RECIPES
for EVERY DAY

Aimée Wimbush-Bourque

PHOTOGRAPHY BY Tim *and* Angela Chin

PENGUIN

an imprint of Penguin Canada, a division of
Penguin Random House Canada Limited

Canada • USA • UK • Ireland • Australia •
New Zealand • India • South Africa • China

First published 2017

www.penguinrandomhouse.ca

LIBRARY AND ARCHIVES CANADA
CATALOGUING IN PUBLICATION

Wimbush-Bourque, Aimée, author
    The simple bites kitchen : nourishing whole
food recipes for every day / Aimée Wimbush-Bourque.

ISBN 978-0-14-319051-6 (softcover)
ISBN 978-0-7352-3297-6 (electronic)

1. Cooking (Natural foods). 2. Cookbooks. I. Title.
TX741.W56 2017   641.5'63   C2016-907467-6

Photography by Tim and Angela Chin
Food and prop styling by Aimée Wimbush-Bourque
Cover and interior design by Five Seventeen

Printed and bound in China

10 9 8 7 6 5 4 3 2 1

For the readers of
Simple Bites,
with gratitude for your
support and encouragement.

Contents

Introduction

You'd think after all the time I've spent working in the food industry, as well as writing the *Simple Bites* food blog and two cookbooks, people would believe me when I say that the kitchen is my favourite place in the home. Yet I still have to convince many that cooking isn't a chore for me—it's an act of love. For me, preparing food is one of the most familiar and natural gestures of caring for my family.

I remember once returning home from a short solo trip and being shyly informed by my son Mateo: "I've missed your hugs and your *food*. Daddy's food is good, but I think you put more love into yours." What an intuitive observation from an eight-year-old! I like to think he could *taste* the love being passed through my cooking.

My kitchen is spacious and functional, open at both ends for smooth traffic flow, and it has plenty of counter space. Despite all this, it isn't quite my dream space. It was renovated before we bought the house, and the upgrade came with ugly countertops and altogether too many warm tones from floor to ceiling. However, the practical side of me won't fix what isn't broke, and so I choose to focus on the positive aspects of my kitchen.

Two large windows look out onto the lane in front of our house and the woods beyond; afternoon sun fills the space with light, and I bask in that much-needed sunshine when I'm prepping dinner. Looking out those windows, I can spot my children hopping off the school bus and tearing home across the lawn. In my kitchen there is always room for my children to join me, and they do after school, with floury aprons and expectations of good things to come. It is their space as much as it is mine—the true heart of the home.

While my kitchen may not be the most modern, by golly, it's always toasty warm in winter and cool in summer. There are cupboards enough to hold my slow cooker and ice cream machine, and a tall pantry for my stash of home preserves. And for the first time in my life I have matching appliances and a refrigerator that doesn't freeze my produce. This kitchen has been my ground control for launching so many projects, from an award-winning blog to a bestselling cookbook, a vibrant Instagram feed and, once upon a time, a backyard wedding.

In this, my second cookbook, I'd once again like to invite you to join me in my kitchen; think of it as a behind-the-scenes personal tour, with recipes and stories. We'll peek in my refrigerator (page 16), pack a lunch box shoulder to shoulder (page 63), throw a feast on the patio and host a pie social (page 179).

We'll gather around the dinner table and talk about healthy family food habits (page 9). Together we'll invest some quality kitchen time to learn a few basics, such as how to cook pulses (page 237), and I'll even talk you through how to preserve the bounty of the season without canning (page 259). It's going to be such fun! So tie on an apron and come on in.

⁂

The recipes in this book reflect how my family eats every day. To keep us all healthy, I focus on serving nutritious food—unprocessed, unrefined, fresh, organic when possible, vegetarian most days, homemade when we can.

We eat a flexitarian diet, with everything in moderation, focusing on whole ingredients while reducing our meat intake. Along the way there are very few restrictions, yet we strive for balance. We embrace glorious imports such as coffee, chocolate and Meyer lemons, but balance them out with ingredients from the many nearby farms, as well as produce and eggs from our own homestead.

The wide variety of food produced in this vast country has enchanted me ever since I was little. As a wee one alongside my older brother, I slung a fishing line over the side of a canoe, hoping to nab some lake trout, and I foraged for wild strawberries and morels to bring back to my mother's kitchen. I've watched wild salmon spawn on the west coast and I've dug for clams on the east coast; each year my culinary education continues to expand. One recent summer I had the opportunity to travel to a family-owned lentil farm in Saskatchewan. Another journey took me to the Discovery Islands in British Columbia, where wild blackberries and fresh oysters are plentiful in July. These experiences influence how I approach family food and inspire me to seek out local foods and prepare them as simply as possible.

You'll find that my recipes are nutrient-dense, fairly simple and utterly delicious. Most of them are not developed specifically for children, but all the dishes are kid-approved by one or all of my little ones. Along with over 100 wholesome recipes, you'll find loads of kitchen tips, advice on cooking with kids, simple tutorials and inspiration for unconventional hospitality.

If you are familiar with my *Simple Bites* blog and Instagram feed, then the recipes in this book will feel like an extension of my online work. Every recipe has a photo and every image was photographed in and around my kitchen. I cooked each dish and baked every item myself. I styled the food simply in hopes that the recipes will come across as approachable rather than daunting.

As you cook for your family, I'd like to join you in the kitchen as a friend and fellow parent. It is my wish that this book, in its humble way, may inspire you to expand your repertoire and further nourish your family, one recipe and one meal at a time. Please drop me a note at aimee@simplebites.net and share your experiences from using this cookbook. I'd love to hear from you.

My Childhood Kitchen

I suppose I am easy to please when it comes to home kitchens. I just have to think back to the rural kitchen where I grew up as a homesteader in the Yukon Territory to realize how luxurious my current space really is. Back then, cooking was an adventure, not too different from the way Ma Ingalls or Marilla Cuthbert ran *their* kitchens.

Even though my family left our homestead in the Yukon wilderness more than twenty-five years ago, I can still close my eyes and be transported back to that kitchen where my culinary journey began. It's easiest to recall the warm summer days, perhaps because they were so cherished in a place that spent eight or nine months of the year swathed in snow.

Ah, the windows are propped open to let in the lake breeze, as well as the calls of the seagulls and the scent of the wild roses in bloom. Out over the garden and beyond the small greenhouse, I can see the gentle ripples of Jackfish Bay. If I get too hot working over the stove, I'll slip out down to the pebbly lakeshore and go wading in the shallows. I'll bring a pail for water, because along the way, past the clothesline and the rabbit hutches, is a natural spring, and in the summer we draw our drinking water from its cool abundance. If I need hot water for washing up, I'll dip into the rectangular copper boiler that sits perpetually on top of our wood stove. The boiler holds lake water, hauled in year round, even when we have to maintain a hole in the ice, and we keep it heated for both baths and dishes.

Everything my family and I prepare is mixed, kneaded, chopped and grated by hand, from bread dough to stews. We whip cream with a whisk and use a sturdy chef's knife for most tasks. There are no appliances in our kitchen, save for a four-burner propane stove and oven. My mother does have a small hand-cranked pasta machine, and I love to turn out fresh lasagna sheets and great lengths of fettuccine made with our fresh eggs.

I've just strained the goat milk from the morning's milking and need to get it into our cold cellar. It's simply a dirt hole, about nine feet deep in the ground, accessed by a trap door in the Mediterranean-blue tiles of our kitchen floor. We store our dairy down there—homemade yogurt, goat milk and fresh ricotta—as well as eggs. We don't store produce in the cellar; we harvest just enough from our garden for each meal. I draw up a sturdy bucket on a rope and carefully place the jars of fresh milk inside it. My toddler sister, Miranda, kneels next to me and peers down into the "Big Hole" as she calls it. She chatters away unintelligibly to her imaginary friend, Iiddy, who apparently lives in our cold cellar. I hope Iiddy isn't afraid of mice.

This morning my mother will start a rabbit stew on the propane burner and then move it to the back of the wood stove for a slow cook. We keep a chest freezer at our neighbour's farm, about fifteen kilometres away, where they have electricity, and space in one of their elk barns. All year round, we stop in for frozen berries, lake trout fillets, moose meat, goat, rabbit and vegetables put up from the garden. It requires a little planning, but it works for our family.

My older sister has bread rising by the time I have washed and dried the breakfast dishes. After that, the day is ours, to meet our friends on the bluff and hunt for wild berries or to take the canoe out onto the bay and simply drift. Whatever adventures the day brings, I know I'll return to the kitchen in the afternoon to bake up something for dessert. After all, I have the sweet tooth in the family, and the kitchen is my home.

Healthy Family Food Habits

"The shared meal is no small thing. It is a foundation of family life, the place where our children learn the art of conversation and acquire the habits of civilization: sharing, listening, taking turns, navigating differences, arguing without offending."
MICHAEL POLLAN, *Cooked: A Natural History of Transformation*

The family table is where your children will form habits around food that they will take with them into adulthood. The kitchen, the heart of the home, is the birthplace of those habits, habits set in motion by our best intentions as parents. Good habits are worth being intentional over, especially with little ones looking on.

I continually remind myself of this list of little habits because I know they will have a long-lasting positive influence on my family. These aren't resolutions, or even goals, but merely small steps to introduce positive change.

I'm confident you are doing an excellent job around your family table, but perhaps in reading this list, you will find there are one or two practices you could adopt and thereby help shape your family food culture for the better.

1. REDUCE WASTE This one is first for a reason: wasted food makes me squirm. Cook less, if needed, and reduce portion sizes. Freeze or repurpose leftovers and store foods correctly to avoid waste. Talk with your children about global hunger and teach them to truly care about food waste. When feasible, compost kitchen scraps and recycle as much as possible.

2. MENU PLAN You will definitely waste less food if you make a menu plan and buy only what you need. Menu planning also helps to shape nutritious meals for the family table. I follow a loose Monday-to-Friday plan that I pencil out on Sunday afternoons, but you'll find what works for you along the way. Don't wait to get started with menu planning; you'll discover that both sanity and money are saved in the process.

3. REVIEW FOOD VALUES Is eating locally and in season important to you? How can you take steps to improve your food sustainability as a family? We grow some of our own produce and round out what we need from local farmers. I'm also a member of a winter CSA so that the majority of our produce from November to May is grown nearby (in rooftop greenhouses) and travels only a few short kilometres to our table. It's important to us to support local growers as well as be conscientious of food miles—the distance food travels to your table.

4. TRUST MORE Delegating kitchen tasks to children gets easier the more you learn to let go. Give them an opportunity to shine, because they will undoubtedly surpass your expectations and the benefits are many. Also, trust yourself more in the kitchen. Try new recipes, new methods and new ingredients. Failure is a sign of action; you'll never grow as a cook without stepping up. Like Julia Child famously said: "Learn how to cook—try new recipes, learn from your mistakes, be fearless, and above all have fun."

5. STRESS LESS Are your children only eating bread? Refusing meat? Gobbling down breakfast but just picking at dinner? These are normal patterns from what I have experienced. If they don't get three square meals every day, don't worry—they'll be fine. Try not to put the kids under any pressure, and instead focus on making those foods they love as nutritious as possible.

6. STOCK UP SMART It's almost too obvious to point out, but if you stock nourishing foods in your kitchen, you'll eat better. Keep out the junk, thus encouraging smart snacking and wholesome family meals. Stock a pantry with real, unprocessed ingredients and let them inspire your cooking.

7. EMBRACE HOSPITALITY Let your children see you open your home and welcome others around your table. Through your actions, they will learn how to be gracious hosts. While you're at it, make a few meals for others and let someone know you are thinking of them. The "Fresh-Air Gatherings" section is packed with recipes to share. Remember, "entertaining" puts the emphasis on you and things like the menu and the decor, but "extending hospitality" shifts the focus to others and meeting their needs graciously.

8. PRACTISE BALANCE Moderation is a foreign concept to children, yet never has it been more important that they learn it, with junk foods now so widely promoted. Don't deprive them of treats entirely, but lead by example in demonstrating that a little goes a long way.

9. ENCOURAGE CONVERSATION Connecting with one another around the table is one of the main reasons why we gather as a family. Listen. Ask questions. Talk about stuff that matters and show the children you are truly interested. Spark conversation in your more reluctant talkers by playing "Tall Tales" for fun: each person around the table takes a turn sharing three things about their day but with one of them being a tall tale, then the others around the table must guess which one isn't true.

10. SHOW THANKFULNESS Slow down long enough to acknowledge the food in front of you before you eat. Perhaps say a prayer or a few words of gratitude. When so many in the world go hungry, it's important to reflect on our abundance.

Kids in the Kitchen

At some point in my early years of being a mother, I figured out that it was easier to welcome my children into the kitchen than shoo them out to potentially get into mischief. They had already realized that if they wanted to spend time with me, it was going to be at the counter or the stove—the bonus was that deliciousness was bound to ensue.

The kitchen has long been my preferred place in the home, and so it is only natural that my three children—Noah (twelve), Mateo (nine) and Clara (five)—should learn to love it at an early age, too. I am nearly always in the kitchen, and they gravitate to my side, following in a clear set of footprints that lead toward self-sufficiency. Together we measure and stir, roll and bake, all the while learning, laughing and strengthening our relationships.

Laying a foundation for a healthy family food culture starts with simple food prep and a willingness on your part to invest the time in teaching kids when they are so impressionable. To me, it's never too early to get kids into the kitchen, and my three have all cut their cooking teeth alongside me from as young as two. I think it's important to encourage an interest in food and cooking right from toddlerhood. No, we don't hand over small appliances for them to use, but by letting them measure and stir, we build their confidence and encourage participation.

My children join me in the kitchen each in their own way, and this is important to recognize in your own children. They may have no interest in cooking, or they may take an approach that is the complete opposite of yours. Remember that all children are different, and interest levels and attention spans vary vastly. You'll know just how much to attempt with your child.

In our home, Noah is the planner; he flips through a cookbook or magazine and gets inspired. He assembles ingredients and sees a project through to completion—or consumption, rather. Mateo sails through the kitchen, skids to a stop and demands, "Hey, can I do that?" He'll stick around for a task (and a taste) or two before vanishing, chasing another idea that strikes his fancy. Clara pushes a chair up to the counter and asks, "What can I do for you?" She waits for instruction, and is happy with most any task as long as we're doing it together. She's confident, and loves to inform me that she is *very* good at this job or that, just in case I had forgotten. Noah would rather use a knife than a rolling pin, while Mateo loves mixing pizza dough or pita bread (page 68) with his hands. Mateo doesn't have the patience for grating, but Noah steadily sees the job through. Together, we all get the work done and get dinner on the table.

In the kitchen, I believe that the most important thing for children to know is that they are welcome. Everything else can be taught, but the feeling of belonging must be impressed upon them from the beginning. Keep this up and eventually cooking from scratch will be second nature to them and ignite a love of nourishing, real food that will last a lifetime.

∼ 8 Steps for When Kids Cook ∼

1. Wash your hands!

2. Read the recipe completely.

3. Assemble the required tools.

4. Assemble the ingredients.

5. Follow the instructions in the recipe.

6. Work safely.

7. Serve and share the dish.

8. Clean up the kitchen!

SPRING   SUMMER

The Fine Art of Fridge Management

Fridge management is a real thing. Some call it rotation or organization, but it simply means letting your fridge live up to its potential. With a little planning and discipline, you can shop smarter, waste less and eat better year round.

While I will sing the praises of a well-stocked pantry all the livelong day, I do not echo the same sentiments when it comes to the refrigerator. I believe it is better to keep the fridge slightly below full, but never stuffed—except at holidays, of course! This way you can easily see to the back and take note of what needs to be consumed.

Being able to see at a glance the contents of your fridge is important. It helps you to stay motivated to use up what you have instead of going shopping. Storing foods in jars to keep them visible is practical. Also, a clean, airtight container like a jar will keep your food fresher for much longer than a hastily plastic-covered bowl or a loose produce bag.

Homemade soups, grain salads, preserves, condiments, sauces and much more—if they work in a jar, they go in a jar. Keep on hand a good stash of flip-top jars (also known as French canning jars) and wide-mouth jars.

I'm so averse to wasting food that my refrigerator is one of the cleanest places in my home. At least once a week, challenge yourself to a fridge-only meal—perhaps a Quick Crustless Ham and Cheese Quiche (page 206) or an enormous salad. Use up ends of cheese, cooked meats or roasted vegetables in my Every-Season Risotto (page 189). And don't forget about making a Basic Vegetable Stock (page 231) for all the odds and ends from the crisper drawers.

Empty the fridge at least once a month so you can wipe down shelves and remove unseen bacteria. Cleaning out drawers will force you to turn withering produce into soup and turn tired apples into a comforting Roasted Apple and Ginger Tisane (page 56).

Incorporate leftovers into your loose menu for the week, instead of shoving them to the back of the refrigerator. Make Whole Simmered Chicken (page 213) one day and use what's left in my Tangy Quinoa Carrot Chicken Salad (page 75) a day or two later. Enjoy Roast Beef (page 208) the night you cook it, then slice leftovers for sandwiches with Green Olive Tapenade (page 76). Leftover roasted vegetables are featured in a Roasted Sweet Potato, Pesto and Bacon Wrap (page 78). If you're smart about it, you can have a week's worth of lunches and dinners at your fingertips.

Nourishing Breakfasts

It is debatable whether I am a morning person, but I am a confirmed breakfast enthusiast. I have always been in the camp that regards breakfast as the most important meal of the day, and now health professionals have significant research to confirm this theory. Is a nourishing breakfast the secret to staying healthy? I believe it is one of the main contributors to a balanced diet and long-term health—but not just any breakfast.

In the hustle and bustle of life, breakfast for many people nowadays is a sugary cereal shaken out of a box. Yet it can be so much more. With a jar of my homemade muesli or a batch of whole-grain waffles warmed from the freezer and paired with fresh fruit, I can get a nourishing breakfast on the table in seconds. The first order of the day, however, is always a tall glass of room-temperature water with a squeeze of lemon to rehydrate after my night's sleep. I recommend this simple morning routine for all ages, as it will boost your metabolic rate and start your day off on the right foot.

Black coffee is another constant of mine, and big pots of hot cereals are in regular rotation in the Simple Bites kitchen. I grew up eating them back on our Yukon homestead, and my children love them as well. We simmer millet, cornmeal and oats of all kinds, serve them up savoury or sweet, dished into five big bowls on our farmhouse table. Cold cereal only shows up on the occasional camping trip or when Mama is out of town. It's not forbidden, but it's not a fallback either. Many of the health issues that plague the modern world are linked to packaged and processed foods; we certainly can do better than starting our day with a box of cereal.

On the busiest of mornings, we serve ourselves homemade Brown Sugar Cinnamon Instant Oatmeal (page 48) or Apple Crisp Muesli Mix (page 25) and top it with yogurt or Coconut Almond Milk (page 227) for a fast bite. I set out a fruit bowl that changes with the seasons, and the kids help themselves. For three seasons of the year our chickens give us six brown eggs a day, which I cook up into frittatas or fry for my Egg-Topped Umami Oatmeal (page 47).

Of course we must make place for maple syrup, the sweetest way to eat local in Quebec. My children all inherited the ability to roll out of bed and inhale a stack of waffles or a plate of eggs. Spinach Crêpes with Blueberry Compote (page 32), Whole-Grain Gingerbread Waffles with Molasses Cinnamon Syrup (page 44) and my son's specialty, Noah's French Toast with Cinnamon Maple Butter (page 42), are all favourites for weekends when we have time to linger around the table.

If I've invited friends over for brunch, I'll likely bake a batch of Spelt Date Scones (page 35) or Overnight Spiced Stollen Swirl Buns (page 37), especially if it's around the winter holidays. My Winter Citrus and Cranberry Salad (page 55) and a bowl of soft scrambled eggs would round out the meal.

Most mornings the whole family can be found in the kitchen prepping our first meal of the day. Danny is stationed at the espresso machine, pulling my Americano, and I am at the stove, stirring the hot cereal. Noah feeds the cats and then joins us, always the sleepyhead. Clara sets the table, and Mateo helps by pouring juice and doling out multivitamins.

It's just as important for us to start our day together as it is to finish it together at the dinner table. Whether breakfast is rushed or relaxed, it's part of our routine, and we never miss a day.

KIDS IN THE BREAKFAST KITCHEN

Most weekday mornings, my children are eager to get in the kitchen to mix
and whip, bake and serve. It's a good time to teach them the basics, in a relaxed
environment where no one has to rush out the door to school or work. In fact,
I recommend breakfast as the best meal to get your kids cooking by themselves.
Start simple, of course, with dishes like fruit salad, scrambled eggs and buttered

toast. Before long they will be ready to move on to simple pancakes, Noah's French Toast with Cinnamon Maple Butter (page 42) and more.

This brings to mind one particular morning when my boys, then six and eight, decided to prepare a pancake breakfast all on their own. It was the morning of our wedding anniversary. The evening before had been full of fugitive huddles and fervent whispers between brothers. Now we were instructed to remain in bed, and coffee arrived fairly quickly. Noah was wincing a little because he had splashed some on his bare foot, but "Mom, I stayed calm anyway," he reported.

"We're making pancakes!" Mateo announced, jumping from one foot to the other. I raised my eyebrows and then shrugged. "Okay. Let me know if you need help."

They took Clara back downstairs with them and gave her juice and toast (she wakes up ravenous) to keep her busy. I could hear Mateo chirping at her, while Noah got to work making the pancake batter. Eventually they invited us downstairs, where Mateo had set the table and had whipped cream by hand. Noah fried a platter of pancakes and had even trekked to the garden to get a fistful of flowers for the table. There was a glass of juice at every place setting and cloth napkins, too. It was all so warm and inviting, my heart swelled with the sweetness of their gestures. And it must be stated that the morning's collaboration had been squabble-free.

We took our time around the table, laughing and eating up every single pancake and sipping our juice. Even the whipped cream disappeared. Both boys were practically levitating with pride, which was precious to see.

I noticed a long plastic straw in the 1 litre mason jar that held our morning orange juice. When I inquired about it, Noah looked a little uncomfortable, but then revealed that he hadn't known how to pour from the jar without spilling it. He confessed he had used the straw to suck the juice out of the jar and then spit it out into our glasses to fill them.

Oh, how we roared with laughter! Oh, how his engineer father praised his ingenuity and ability to solve a problem. And oh, how our friends laughed when we shared the slightly gruesome story later. Even though I unknowingly drank my son's spittle, that morning was still perfect—and one I will always remember. It encouraged me to hand over to my children even more responsibility in the kitchen, confident they could not only take charge but problem solve along the way, too.

Apple Crisp Muesli Mix

MAKES 12 CUPS (2.8 L), 6 TO 8 SERVINGS

Dried apples, cinnamon-toasted oats and puffed ancient grains make up the bulk of this hearty cold cereal. Almonds give a much-needed energy boost in the morning, but feel free to use any nuts you have on hand, or omit them for a nut-free version. I adore this with a splash of chilled Coconut Almond Milk (page 227) and sliced persimmon, but Danny insists it is best sprinkled over plain yogurt and topped with fresh berries. In this, we agree to disagree.

A jar of this muesli mix makes a lovely gift with a pint of just-picked berries, but you might not want to part ways with your new favourite breakfast cereal.

2½ cups (625 mL) old-fashioned rolled oats

1 cup (250 mL) large unsweetened coconut flakes

1 cup (250 mL) raw pepitas

⅔ cup (150 mL) raw sunflower seeds

⅔ cup (150 mL) slivered almonds

½ cup (125 mL) fresh-pressed apple juice

1 teaspoon (5 mL) ground cinnamon

2 cups (500 mL) chopped dried apples

2 cups (500 mL) puffed quinoa

2 cups (500 mL) puffed millet

2 cups (500 mL) puffed rice

1. Preheat oven to 325°F (160°C). Line two rimmed baking sheets with parchment paper and position the oven racks to the upper and lower thirds.

2. In a medium bowl, stir together oats, coconut flakes, pepitas, sunflower seeds and almonds.

3. Measure the apple juice, add the cinnamon and stir with a fork to combine. Pour the juice over the muesli mix. Toss well to coat the dry ingredients with the juice.

4. Spread the muesli in a thin layer on the prepared baking sheets. Toast in the oven for 30 minutes, stirring occasionally. Muesli will turn slightly golden but should not get too dark. Transfer muesli to a large bowl and cool completely.

5. Add the dried apples, quinoa, millet and rice and toss well to combine. Transfer to a large jar or airtight container and store at room temperature for up to 3 weeks.

Broiled Grapefruit with Coconut Sugar

I was dubious about broiled grapefruit for most of my life until cookbook author Alana Chernila set a platter of warm, ruby-red grapefruit in front of me one morning at brunch. That settled it. If Alana deemed them worthy of attention, then they must be remarkable. Of course they were, and broiled grapefruit are now a winter staple around my table.

I've experimented with nearly every natural sweetener, and I love to top my grapefruit with coconut sugar the most. It turns sticky and dark when caramelized under the broiler. If you don't have coconut sugar on hand, substitute any brown sugar such as Demerara or muscovado.

2 pink grapefruit

4 teaspoons (20 mL) coconut sugar

¼ teaspoon (1 mL) ground cinnamon

1 teaspoon (5 mL) salted butter

1. Preheat broiler to 500°F (260°C).

2. With a sharp knife, shave off ¼ inch (5 mm) of peel from the top and bottom of each grapefruit so the halves will stand upright. Slice each grapefruit in half along its equator. With a small serrated knife, cut around the grapefruit segments to loosen them from the membrane and the peel; discard any visible seeds.

3. In a small bowl, stir together coconut sugar and cinnamon. Place the grapefruit halves cut side up in a small baking pan and sprinkle each half with 1 teaspoon (5 mL) of the sugar mixture. Dot grapefruit halves with butter.

4. Broil grapefruit for 4 to 5 minutes, until sugar is slightly caramelized. Keep a close eye on them so that they don't burn. Cool slightly before serving in shallow bowls with a spoon.

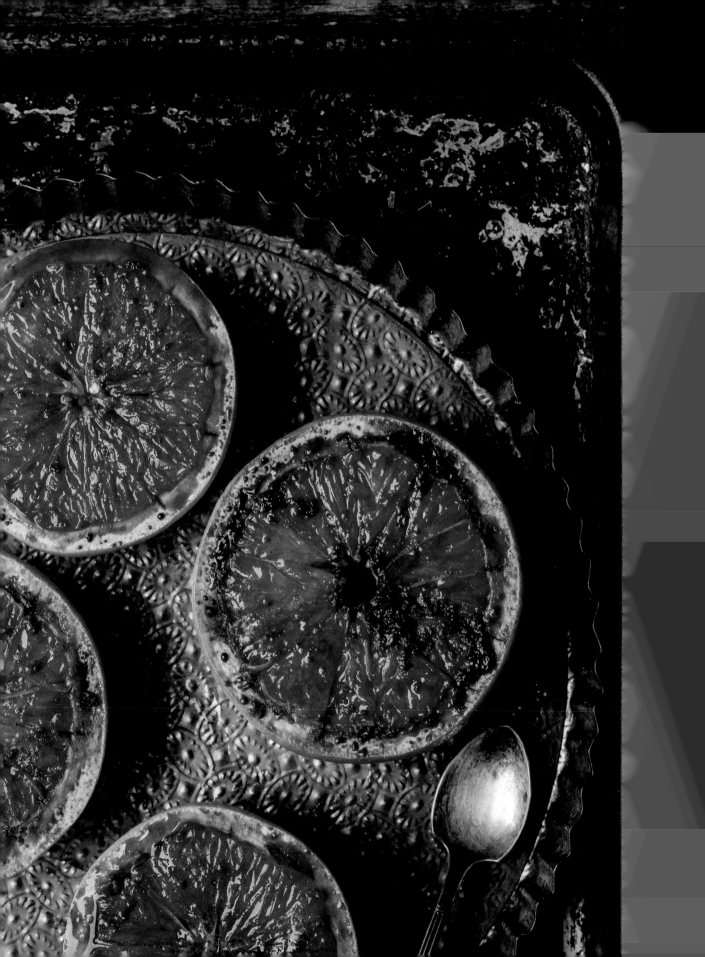

Maple-Roasted Pears with Granola

SERVES 4

My breakfast frequently consists of fruit, grains and yogurt, and this recipe contains all three, married with a generous pour of that prized local condiment, maple syrup. I roast halved pears until tender and top them with crunchy pecan-studded granola for a decadent yet simple breakfast. Clumps of my own maple-sweetened granola work well in this dish, but you can use any granola you have on hand.

This dish makes an easy jump to dessert: just skip the yogurt topping and add a scoop of vanilla ice cream instead.

2 large pears, such as Bartlett, Anjou or Bosc, washed

2 teaspoons (10 mL) salted butter, melted

4 tablespoons (60 mL) pure maple syrup, divided

1 cup (250 mL) Granola Cluster Trail Mix (page 95) or your favourite granola

¼ cup (60 mL) pecans, chopped

1 cup (250 mL) full-fat organic plain yogurt, for serving

1. Preheat oven to 375°F (190°C).

2. Cut pears in half lengthwise. Scoop out the cores with a small spoon or a melon baller. Arrange pears cut side up in a pie plate.

3. Swirl the melted butter and 1 tablespoon (15 mL) of the maple syrup together in a small bowl. Brush generously onto the pears. Roast for 20 minutes, or until pears are soft when gently poked with a fork.

4. Combine Granola Cluster Trail Mix (without the add-ins, just the granola clusters), chopped pecans and remaining 3 tablespoons (45 mL) maple syrup in a small bowl. Remove pears from the oven and mound granola into the cavity and over the top of the pears. A packed ice cream scoop works well for this task. It's okay if the granola mixture spills down the sides.

5. Return the pan to the oven and roast for another 5 minutes to toast the granola. Serve immediately with a dollop of yogurt on top.

Asparagus Cheddar Frittata

SERVES 4

❧

Get a big helping of vegetables in the morning, along with a serious protein boost, in this beloved recipe featuring fresh eggs and seasonal asparagus. Chives, asparagus and arugula are all spring produce here in Quebec, which makes them an obvious pairing in this dish. When ramps sprout in my wild garden in May, I use them in place of the chives to give the frittata a mild garlic kick.

Change up the topping with your favourite microgreen, lettuce, sprouts or spinach. For special occasions, such as Easter brunch, serve the frittata alongside thin shavings of Gin-Cured Gravlax (page 151). Breakfast doesn't get much better, in my opinion.

1 pound (450 g) asparagus (18 to 20 medium spears)

2 tablespoons (30 mL) extra-virgin olive oil, divided

8 large eggs

2 tablespoons (30 mL) chopped fresh chives

1 tablespoon (15 mL) water

½ teaspoon (2 mL) sea salt

1½ cups (375 mL) grated sharp cheddar cheese

4 cups (1 L) baby arugula

½ teaspoon (2 mL) balsamic vinegar

Dash each of sea salt and freshly ground black pepper

2 tablespoons (30 mL) toasted pine nuts

1. Lightly oil a 9-inch (23 cm) skillet or oven-safe sauté pan.

2. Peel the bottom two-thirds of the asparagus and snap off the woody ends. Pieces should be 4 to 5 inches (10 to 12 cm) long.

3. Add 1 tablespoon (15 mL) of the olive oil to the skillet and heat over medium heat. Tumble in the asparagus and cook, stirring occasionally, for 2 to 3 minutes while you prepare the eggs.

4. In a medium bowl, beat together eggs, chives, water and salt until just combined. Do not over-beat.

5. Pour eggs over the asparagus and reduce heat to low. Sprinkle the grated cheese over the eggs. Partially cover the skillet and gently cook for 5 minutes, or until the eggs have solidified. Meanwhile, preheat broiler to 500°F (260°C).

6. Slide the frittata under the broiler for about a minute, until the cheese is bubbly and golden brown. Remove pan and cool slightly.

7. In a large bowl, toss arugula with the remaining 1 tablespoon (15 mL) olive oil, balsamic vinegar and salt and pepper. Heap onto the frittata and finish with the toasted pine nuts. Slice frittata into 4 portions and serve warm.

Spinach Crêpes with Blueberry Compote

SERVES 4 · REQUIRES TIME FOR PREP

My kids call these "Hulk Crêpes," and they were a hit from the moment I tossed wilted spinach into the blender with my batter and fried up bright green crêpes for breakfast. Of course these can be topped with anything you like, but we're particularly fond of pairing them with wild blueberry compote. Use fresh or frozen blueberries for the compote. For a special treat, try the crêpes stuffed with Lighter Ricotta (page 224).

The batter needs to rest in the refrigerator for a while, so plan accordingly. It can be prepared the evening before, so all you have to do in the morning is fry the crêpes.

Spinach crêpes

4 tablespoons (60 mL) unsalted butter, melted, divided, plus more for cooking the crêpes

3 cups (750 mL) packed baby spinach

3 large eggs

1 cup (250 mL) all-purpose flour

1½ cups (375 mL) 2% milk or leftover whey from Lighter Ricotta (page 224)

2 teaspoons (10 mL) raw cane sugar

1 teaspoon (5 mL) pure vanilla extract

½ teaspoon (2 mL) sea salt

Blueberry compote

1 tablespoon (15 mL) salted butter

1 cup (250 mL) fresh or frozen blueberries

2 tablespoons (30 mL) pure maple syrup

A squeeze of fresh lemon

1. **MAKE THE SPINACH CRÊPES** Heat 1 tablespoon (15 mL) of the melted butter in a sauté pan over medium-high heat until bubbly. Add spinach and sauté, stirring continually, for about a minute, until slightly wilted. Remove from heat and cool slightly.

2. Crack the eggs into a bowl, then transfer them to a blender. Whip until frothy. Add the warm spinach and blend until liquefied.

3. Add the flour and blend again. Stop the blender and scrape down the sides. Add the milk, sugar, vanilla and salt; blend until smooth. Add the remaining 3 tablespoons (45 mL) melted butter and blend for an additional minute.

4. Place the blender jug in the refrigerator and chill the batter for at least 2 hours or overnight.

5. When you're ready to cook, briefly blend the batter one more time, as it will have separated.

6. Heat an 8- or 10-inch (20 or 25 cm) nonstick pan over medium heat. Brush pan with some melted butter and pour a scant ¼ cup (60 mL) of batter into the middle. Immediately lift the pan and tilt in a circular motion so the batter coats the pan in a circle. Cook for about 1 minute, until the edges are light golden.

7. Slip a flexible spatula under the crêpe and flip it with a delicate hand. Cook for an additional 30 seconds, then remove to a plate and fold into quarters. Keep warm under a clean tea towel. Repeat until all the crêpes are cooked.

8. **MAKE THE BLUEBERRY COMPOTE** In a small saucepan over medium heat, melt the butter. Add the blueberries and cook for 4 to 5 minutes, longer if the berries were frozen, stirring occasionally until the berries soften and turn blue-black. Stir in the maple syrup and add a squeeze of lemon. Cook the sauce for an additional minute, then remove from heat and spoon over crêpes.

Spelt Date Scones

MAKES 12 LARGE SCONES

When fresh berries are out of season, dates are my first pick for adding a little excitement to a breakfast scone. Medjool dates are the best choice, leaving little pockets of sweetness throughout the soft dough. Spelt is one of the lighter whole-grain flours and my preferred choice for fluffy yet filling scones. These are delicious with a smear of butter and a spoonful of Spiced Pear Jam with Bourbon (page 286).

This recipe makes a big batch, enough to serve if friends are over for brunch, so go ahead and put on a big pot of coffee. The scones also keep very well: store leftovers in a resealable freezer bag and freeze for up to 3 months.

2½ cups (625 mL) whole spelt flour

2 teaspoons (10 mL) baking powder

½ teaspoon (2 mL) baking soda

½ teaspoon (2 mL) sea salt

4 tablespoons (60 mL) cold unsalted butter

8 Medjool dates, pitted and chopped

2 medium eggs, at room temperature, divided

1 cup (250 mL) sour cream

¼ cup (60 mL) agave syrup

3 tablespoons (45 mL) Homemade Buttermilk (page 228) or store-bought

1 teaspoon (5 mL) pure vanilla extract

1. Preheat oven to 425°F (220°C). Line a rimmed baking sheet with parchment paper.

2. In a large bowl, whisk together flour, baking powder, baking soda and salt. Using the large holes of a box grater, grate the butter into the flour. Rub the butter into the flour with your hands until it resembles coarse cornmeal. Add the chopped dates and toss to coat them thoroughly.

3. In a medium bowl, whisk together 1 egg with the sour cream, agave, Homemade Buttermilk and vanilla. Pour over the dry ingredients and gently fold together with a spatula just until a soft dough forms.

4. Turn dough out onto a floured counter. With floured hands, pat it into an 8-inch (20 cm) circle. With a lightly floured knife, cut dough into 12 wedges. Transfer scones to the baking sheet.

5. Beat remaining egg with a few drops of water and brush onto the tops of the scones. Bake for 14 to 16 minutes, until they spring back when touched and tops are golden brown. Enjoy warm.

Overnight Spiced Stollen Swirl Buns

MAKES 12 BUNS · REQUIRES TIME FOR PREP

When Danny and I were newly married, we didn't have much money for holiday presents, so we made homemade treats as gifts for our loved ones. One year, we worked side by side to produce a dozen large stollen loaves straight out of *Joy of Cooking*. We coated those beauties in powdered sugar, wrapped them in cellophane—and then never made the recipe again.

In recent years, I've been revisiting the comforts of stollen over the winter holidays, but in swirl bun form. A lightly spiced dough, studded with dried cranberries, almonds and a hint of candied orange peel—it's heaven on Christmas morning. I've developed these to be overnight rolls, but you can always do the second rise right after the shaping and bake them right away. Just be sure to enjoy them warm from the oven.

⅔ cup (150 mL) 2% milk

2 teaspoons (10 mL) active dry yeast

3¼ cups (810 mL) all-purpose flour, divided

½ cup (125 mL) unsweetened dried cranberries

3 tablespoons (45 mL) candied orange peel

1 tablespoon (15 mL) rum

¾ cup (175 mL) unsalted butter, softened, divided

¾ cup (175 mL) raw cane sugar, divided

2 large eggs

½ teaspoon (2 mL) fine sea salt

½ teaspoon (2 mL) ground cardamom

1 teaspoon (5 mL) ground cinnamon

½ teaspoon (2 mL) ground allspice

½ cup (125 mL) slivered almonds

Powdered sugar, for dusting

1. Heat the milk in a small saucepan over medium-high heat until scalded, then cool to wrist warm or around 110°F (43°C). Pour into a medium bowl and whisk in the yeast. Let stand for 5 minutes to activate the yeast. Beat in ½ cup (125 mL) of the flour, then cover the bowl with a tea towel and let stand in a warm place while you prepare the rest of the ingredients.

2. In the same saucepan, combine dried cranberries, candied orange peel and rum. Warm gently, then turn off heat and let soak.

3. In the bowl of a stand mixer fitted with the paddle attachment, cream ½ cup (125 mL) of the soft butter with ½ cup (125 mL) of the sugar until light and fluffy. Beat in the eggs, one at a time, followed by the salt and cardamom. Tip in the yeast sponge and add ½ cup (125 mL) of the flour. Mix on low speed until the dough comes together.

(recipe continues)

4. Switch to the dough hook and add the remaining 2¼ cups (550 mL) flour, ½ cup (125 mL) at a time, mixing on low speed until a soft dough forms. Knead on low speed for 5 minutes. Remove the dough hook, cover the dough with a tea towel and let rise in a warm place for 1 hour or until doubled in size.

5. On a lightly floured counter, roll out dough to a 12- × 16-inch (30 × 40 cm) rectangle. Spread the remaining ¼ cup (60 mL) soft butter in an even layer over the dough, going right to the edges. Mix the remaining ¼ cup (60 mL) sugar with cinnamon and allspice, then sprinkle evenly over the butter. Evenly scatter slivered almonds and soaked fruit over the buttered dough. Starting from a short end, tightly roll the dough into a log. Using a sharp knife, cut the dough into 12 buns, each 1 inch (2.5 cm) thick. Gently reshape them into rounds if they get overly squashed.

6. Butter two 13- × 18-inch (32 × 40 cm) rimmed baking sheets. Place 6 buns on each sheet and cover loosely with plastic wrap. Refrigerate overnight.

7. In the morning, allow the buns to rise in a warm place for about 1½ hours or until doubled in size. You can do this step in the oven, with the oven turned off but the oven light turned on. If you do this, make sure to remove them before preheating the oven.

8. Preheat oven to 350°F (180°C) and position oven racks in the upper and lower thirds of the oven. Remove plastic wrap and bake buns for 22 to 24 minutes, rotating once, until golden brown. Dust with powdered sugar and serve warm.

Honey Whole Wheat Bagels

Growing up so far north, in the Yukon, meant we lived without ready access to many of life's little pleasures. Great croissants, baguettes and bagels were just some of the things we couldn't buy, and so from as far back as I can remember, we made our own. My sister and I perfected our bagel recipe and technique so well we'd sell out every Saturday at our family's booth in the local farmer's market.

Even though I now live thirty minutes from the best fresh bagels in North America, I haven't given up making my homemade bagels. These days, my children join me in the kitchen to sling dough and sprinkle the tops with seeds. I've also adapted the recipe to be half whole wheat, which makes them slightly more robust and full-flavoured. No matter where you live, these bagels are sure to become a family favourite in your home, as they have been in ours for generations.

2¼ cups (550 mL) warm water
(105 to 115°F/38 to 40°C)

2 tablespoons (30 mL) active dry
yeast

3 tablespoons (45 mL) liquid
honey

2 teaspoons (10 mL) sea salt

3 cups (750 mL) whole wheat
bread flour

3 cups (750 mL) all-purpose flour

1 tablespoon (15 mL) raw cane
sugar

2 tablespoons (30 mL) fine
cornmeal

1 egg white, beaten with
1 teaspoon (5 mL) water, for
the glaze

Topping options: coarse sea salt;
sesame seeds; poppy seeds;
minced raw onions

1. In the bowl of a stand mixer, combine warm water and yeast. Stir with a fork and leave to sit for about 10 minutes. Add honey, salt and whole wheat flour. Using the paddle attachment, beat mixture on low speed for 1 minute to combine, then beat on high speed for 3 minutes. Turn off the mixer and allow batter to rest for 5 minutes so that the whole wheat flour can absorb the water.

2. Add the all-purpose flour, 1 cup (250 mL) at a time, mixing dough on low speed. The dough will be quite soft. Switch to the dough hook and knead on low speed for 8 minutes. Stop the mixer and scrape down the dough hook or the sides of the bowl as needed. Cover the bowl with plastic wrap and allow the dough to rise for 1 hour or until doubled in size.

3. Meanwhile, position oven racks in the upper and lower thirds of the oven and preheat oven to 450°F (230°C). Lightly oil two rimmed baking sheets and sprinkle with the cornmeal.

(recipe continues)

4. Near the end of the rising period, fill a large pot (at least 4½ quarts/4.2 L) with water. Bring to a boil, then add cane sugar. (The sweetener will give the bagels a nice sheen.) Reduce heat to low and cover the pot.

5. Turn dough out onto a lightly floured counter and punch down. With a sharp knife, divide the dough into 16 equal pieces. Shape each piece into a ball. Allow to rest for 3 or 4 minutes. With your thumb, press deep into the ball to make a hole. Hook the bagel onto the forefinger and index finger of one hand and lift it off the counter. Place the same fingers of your other hand also in the hole and rotate both sets of fingers around each other, gently stretching the dough apart and shaping the bagel.

6. Place formed bagels on a well-floured counter, cover with a tea towel and leave until dough is slightly raised, about 10 minutes. Meanwhile, bring your water back to a low boil.

7. Gently lift bagels, one at a time, and lower into the simmering water. Do not boil more than 3 at a time. Boil for about 60 seconds, then flip them over in the water using a slotted spoon or a spider and boil for another 60 seconds.

8. Lift bagels out with the slotted spoon, drain and place on the baking sheets. Repeat until all the bagels are boiled. Brush with the egg glaze and dress them up with the topping of your choice and a sprinkling of sea salt.

9. Bake bagels for 25 to 30 minutes, until golden brown, rotating the pans halfway through. Cool on a wire rack. Bagels are best enjoyed the day they are made. Any remaining bagels should be frozen in an airtight freezer bag. If you like, slice bagels in half before freezing so they'll toast up faster from frozen.

Noah's French Toast with Cinnamon Maple Butter

SERVES 4

※

A few years ago, just before Mother's Day, I lugged an electric burner and several bags of food and gear to Noah's fourth-grade class and taught a hands-on lesson on how to make beloved French toast. Many of the children had never cracked an egg or whipped cream, not to mention cooked a hot breakfast, but together we completed French toast for the class of twenty-four, topped with maple syrup and mason-jar whipped cream. The whole classroom was pleasantly perfumed with cinnamon, and there were murmurs of pleasure from every corner of the room. I don't know how many kiddos replicated the breakfast for their mother that Sunday, but they all went home with the recipe and full tummies.

Cinnamon maple butter

4 tablespoons (60 mL) salted butter, at room temperature

1 tablespoon (15 mL) pure maple syrup

1 teaspoon (5 mL) ground cinnamon

Noah's French toast

3 large eggs

¾ cup (175 mL) 2% milk

1 tablespoon (15 mL) pure maple syrup

½ teaspoon (2 mL) ground cinnamon, ground nutmeg or Autumn Spice Blend (page 244)

½ teaspoon (2 mL) pure vanilla extract

¼ teaspoon (1 mL) sea salt

Vegetable oil, for cooking

12 slices (1 inch/2.5 cm thick) day-old baguette

Sliced fruit, for garnish

1. **MAKE THE CINNAMON MAPLE BUTTER** In a small bowl, combine the butter, maple syrup and cinnamon. Cream together with a rubber spatula until smooth. Set aside at room temperature.

2. **MAKE NOAH'S FRENCH TOAST** Crack the eggs into a large shallow dish. Add the milk, maple syrup, cinnamon, vanilla and salt and whisk it all together with a fork.

3. Place a large cast-iron or nonstick skillet over medium heat and add enough oil to lightly cover the bottom. You will know that the oil is hot enough when a drop of the egg mixture bubbles in the skillet.

4. When the skillet is nearly hot enough, place 5 or 6 slices of bread in the egg mixture, letting them soak for 30 seconds to 1 minute per side. Using a fork or tongs, carefully transfer the moist bread slices to the skillet. They should sizzle on contact with the skillet.

5. Cook for 1 to 2 minutes, until the underside of each slice is golden. Carefully turn the slices and cook the other side until golden, 1 to 2 minutes more.

6. Place French toast in a pie plate and cover loosely with a clean tea towel to keep warm. Repeat with remaining bread slices. Serve with Cinnamon Maple Butter and sliced fruit.

TIP: *In the classroom that day, I impressed the kids by pouring heavy cream into a chilled pint-size (500 mL) mason jar and shaking it into pillowy perfection. It's not hard to make your own Mason Jar Whipped Cream. Use about ½ cup (125 mL) heavy (35%) cream. Cover tightly with a lid and shake until thick, usually 3 to 4 minutes. Stop shaking when the sloshing subsides. It's best to hold the jar securely by the lid so that your hands don't warm the jar.*

Whole-Grain Gingerbread Waffles with Molasses Cinnamon Syrup

MAKES 6 TO 10 WAFFLES

"I'd say this syrup is as good as Nutella!" Mateo declared one Saturday morning when we were testing this recipe. Beloved gingerbread flavours shine in these wintertime waffles with homemade molasses syrup, as well as the nutty goodness of whole wheat flour and flax. These waffles are substantial enough to keep you full all morning long. The ingredients list may be a bit long, but they are all dry ingredients you probably already have on hand. This recipe will make 6 deep, Belgian-style waffles or about 10 thinner, regular waffles.

Applesauce makes a delicious topping in addition to the Molasses Cinnamon Syrup. And whipping cream is always a good idea.

Molasses cinnamon syrup

¼ cup (60 mL) fancy molasses

¼ cup (60 mL) muscovado or Demerara sugar

2 tablespoons (30 mL) water

¼ teaspoon (1 mL) ground cinnamon or Autumn Spice Blend (page 244)

2 tablespoons (30 mL) unsalted butter

Whole-grain gingerbread waffles

2 large eggs, separated, at room temperature

1½ cups (375 mL) whole wheat pastry flour

¼ cup (60 mL) wheat germ

¼ cup (60 mL) ground flaxseed

¼ cup (60 mL) cornstarch

2 teaspoons (10 mL) baking powder

¼ teaspoon (1 mL) baking soda

½ teaspoon (2 mL) sea salt

½ teaspoon (2 mL) ground ginger

¼ teaspoon (1 mL) freshly grated nutmeg

½ cup (125 mL) pure pumpkin purée

1½ cups (375 mL) 2% milk or whey from Lighter Ricotta (page 244)

4 tablespoons (60 mL) unsalted butter

2 tablespoons (30 mL) liquid honey

1. **MAKE THE MOLASSES CINNAMON SYRUP** In a small pot, combine molasses, sugar, water and cinnamon. Heat, stirring frequently, until the mixture is bubbling slowly and the sugar is dissolved. Whisk in the butter until the syrup is glossy. Set aside and keep warm.

2. **MAKE THE WHOLE-GRAIN GINGERBREAD WAFFLES** Place egg whites in the bowl of a stand mixer fitted with the whisk. Beat on medium-low speed until soft peaks form, about 5 to 6 minutes. Set aside while you prepare the remaining ingredients.

3. In a medium bowl, whisk together flour, wheat germ and flaxseed. Sift in the cornstarch, baking powder, baking soda, salt, ginger and nutmeg. Whisk until well mixed.

4. In a large bowl, whisk the egg yolks and pumpkin purée until creamy. Pour in the milk and whisk again.

5. In a small saucepan over medium heat, melt the butter. Remove from heat and stir in the honey. Whisk into milk mixture.

6. Preheat a waffle iron. Add the dry ingredients to the wet mixture and stir gently to combine. Gently but thoroughly fold in reserved egg whites. Lightly oil the waffle iron. Scoop ¾ cup (175 mL) of the batter and pour into the centre of the waffle iron. Cook for 3½ to 4 minutes, until golden brown and crispy around the edges. Keep warm on a baking sheet in a 150°F (65°C) oven, and then serve waffles with Molasses Cinnamon Syrup.

Egg-Topped Umami Oatmeal

SERVES 4

When I was a child, my dad used to add a splash of soy sauce to his morning bowl of oatmeal. At the time, such a combination was of no interest to me, as I was so content with just a drizzle of honey in mine. However, I now see the appeal of savoury porridge. My dad was on to something with his decidedly bold flavourings first thing in the morning. Starting the day with a healthy bowl of comfort food that satiates your salty and umami cravings is a revelation. I've followed in my dad's footsteps with my own version of his savoury breakfast bowl.

3 teaspoons (15 mL) Golden Ghee (page 223) or extra-virgin olive oil, divided

1 cup (250 mL) steel-cut oats

4 cups (1 L) boiling water

½ teaspoon (2 mL) sea salt

2 cups (500 mL) baby spinach leaves, or to taste

4 tablespoons (60 mL) grated Parmesan cheese, divided

4 eggs (any size)

2 to 4 green onions, thinly sliced

Freshly ground black pepper

1 to 2 teaspoons (5 to 10 mL) tamari soy sauce, or to taste

1. In a medium, heavy saucepan, melt 2 teaspoons (10 mL) of the Golden Ghee over medium heat. Stir in the oats and toast until they smell a bit nutty, about 3 minutes, stirring occasionally. Carefully pour in the boiling water (it will steam vehemently). Increase heat to high and bring to a boil, stirring all the while.

2. When the oats start to really thicken, after 15 minutes or so, sprinkle in the salt. Keep stirring until the oats are creamy and tender, 5 to 7 minutes more. (At this point you can serve up any plain oats for young eaters, because the savoury ingredients are going in next.) Add the spinach leaves and stir until they are wilted. Stir in 2 tablespoons (30 mL) of the Parmesan. Remove from heat and keep warm.

3. Melt the remaining 1 teaspoon (5 mL) Golden Ghee in a nonstick skillet over medium heat. Crack in the eggs and fry until the whites are set but the yolks are still runny.

4. Divide the oatmeal among four bowls. Top with a sprinkling of sliced green onions, black pepper and a drizzle of tamari. Top each serving with an egg. Finish with the remaining 2 tablespoons (30 mL) Parmesan and enjoy at once.

TIP: *Cook the oats ahead of time, store in the refrigerator and warm them up for single servings all week.*

Brown Sugar Cinnamon Instant Oatmeal

This is a recipe to keep in your back pocket year round. It yields a comforting breakfast that is simple to prepare and replaces a popular grocery item with something more nourishing. My children helped me come up with this delicately spiced and lightly sweetened oatmeal. What started as a breakfast food for camping has become a weekday staple that we could happily eat Monday through Friday. Ground chia seeds help to thicken the cereal as well as add an energy boost for the day.

In our freezer there is a half-gallon jar of this mix labelled "Hard Times Oatmeal" because it truly is our backup when Danny or I fall sick or we need a shortcut for some reason. The boys know the ratios by heart and can boil the kettle and get breakfast for themselves and their sister when need be. I recommend you make a double batch of the instant oatmeal mix and store it in a jar on the counter for daily use.

4 cups (1 L) quick-cooking rolled oats, divided	3 tablespoons (45 mL) non-fat powdered milk	½ teaspoon (2 mL) ground cinnamon
½ cup (125 mL) light brown sugar, loosely packed	2 tablespoons (30 mL) ground chia seeds	½ teaspoon (2 mL) sea salt

1. In a food processor, combine 2 cups (500 mL) of the oats, brown sugar, powdered milk, chia seeds, cinnamon and salt. Pulse about 6 or 8 times, until the oats are very finely chopped but not a powder (do not make flour).

2. Add the remaining 2 cups (500 mL) oats and pulse 2 to 3 times to combine.

3. Transfer oatmeal mix to a jar or airtight container and store in a cool, dry place for up to 2 weeks.

4. MAKE THE INSTANT OATMEAL Add ½ cup (125 mL) of oatmeal mix to a bowl or mug and top with 1 cup (250 mL) of boiling water. Stir, cover and let stand for 5 minutes. Stir again and serve.

TIP: *For a delicious maple version, try maple sugar or maple flakes in place of the brown sugar. For a vegan version, omit the powdered milk and finish with a little Coconut Almond Milk (page 227).*

THE SIMPLE BITES KITCHEN

48

Maple Millet Polenta Porridge

SERVES 4 TO 6

As kids, my siblings and I had a nickname for the millet my mother served us for breakfast: gravel. It was never my favourite, but she bought it in bulk and so we had to endure it. Of course she was on to something with millet, because now this gluten-free grain is all the rage, thanks to its heart-healthy properties and delectable nutty flavour.

Since becoming a mother myself, I've revisited this grain and found that partially grinding millet before cooking helps to transform it into a creamy, polenta-like breakfast porridge. It's reminiscent of cream of wheat cereal, but much more flavourful and completely cravable—especially with a drizzle of maple syrup and a heap of fresh fruit.

1 cup (250 mL) millet

1 tablespoon (15 mL) Golden Ghee (page 223) or unsalted butter

2½ cups (625 mL) water

2 cups (500 mL) 2% milk

½ teaspoon (2 mL) sea salt

2 tablespoons (30 mL) pure maple syrup, or to taste

Table (18%) cream, to taste

Fresh fruit such as stone fruit, berries or banana, for garnish

1. Grind millet until it is the texture of coarse cornmeal. I use a blade-type coffee grinder, but a food processor would work.

2. Melt the Golden Ghee in a large, heavy pot over medium-high heat. When it is bubbling, tip in the millet and stir to toast it slightly. Add the water and milk, whisking to eliminate lumps. Bring to a simmer, whisking occasionally, about 5 minutes. The porridge will thicken.

3. Reduce heat to low, cover porridge and cook for 8 minutes without stirring. Stir in the salt and cook, uncovered, for another 5 to 8 minutes, until the porridge is thick and creamy, stirring occasionally to prevent a skin from forming on the top.

4. Turn off heat and cool for a minute. Ladle into bowls and pour over maple syrup. Add a splash of cream, if desired. Top with fresh fruit and serve.

Blushing Apple, Beet and Cherry Smoothie

SERVES 1 · REQUIRES TIME FOR PREP

❧

This smoothie is a healthy and invigorating way to kick-start any day, especially in winter, when fresh produce is scarce. I'm not a big fan of the green smoothie trend (especially in the morning), but this naturally sweet, pretty pink version is one of my favourites. Clara loves it nearly as much as I do, and not just for its vibrant colour. I encourage you to play around with the amount of ginger and turmeric to suit your taste. I'm willing to have their flavours in the forefront because of their many health benefits, but some people find the given amount too strong.

Coconut cream is the thick creamy layer that rises to the top of a can of coconut milk. Refrigerating the can before opening will help the cream to solidify.

1 can (14 ounces/400 mL) full-fat coconut milk

1 small Honeycrisp or Cortland apple, scrubbed, quartered and cored

1 small red beet, scrubbed or peeled

1 cup (250 mL) frozen cherries

2 tablespoons (30 mL) hemp hearts

½ teaspoon (2 mL) grated peeled fresh ginger (about a 1-inch/2.5 cm piece)

½ teaspoon (2 mL) grated peeled fresh turmeric root (about a ½-inch/1 cm piece)

½ cup (125 mL) filtered water

1. Refrigerate the can of coconut milk overnight to solidify the coconut cream.

2. Turn the chilled can of coconut milk upside down (don't shake it) and open the bottom with a can opener. Pour the coconut water into a measuring cup, then scoop out the thickened coconut cream into a small bowl or jar.

3. Chop the apple and the beet into ½-inch (1 cm) chunks and toss them into a high-speed blender. Add the cherries, hemp hearts, ginger, turmeric, filtered water and ½ cup (125 mL) of the coconut water. Blend until smooth. Spoon in 2 tablespoons (30 mL) of the coconut cream and blend until incorporated.

4. Pour into a tall glass or 1-pint (500 mL) jar and serve with a straw.

Winter Citrus and Cranberry Salad

SERVES 4

⚮

In the winter months, when the cravings for fresh fruit kick in, we gravitate toward clementines, oranges and grapefruit. Orange slices sprinkled with cinnamon are a genius palate cleanser in Mexico, and a flavour pairing I love to revisit.

In this salad, a variety of oranges, a drizzle of maple syrup and a sprinkling of cinnamon tease the palate in a refreshing tangy-sweet way. If you have some on hand, try a splash of rosewater instead of cinnamon. And try the salad with pomegranate seeds instead of cranberries for another variation that spotlights winter fruit.

2 clementines or tangerines

4 oranges

½ cup (125 mL) fresh cranberries

2 tablespoons (30 mL) pure maple syrup

½ teaspoon (2 mL) ground cinnamon

½ teaspoon (2 mL) flaky sea salt or Lemon Herb Finishing Salt (page 243)

1. Trim the ends from the clementines and oranges to expose the segments, then cut off the peel and pith from top to bottom. A small serrated knife works best for this task.

2. Slice the fruit into ¼-inch (5 mm) rounds, removing any seeds you encounter. Arrange the rounds on plates or a platter with a slight edge to hold in the juice. Thinly slice the cranberries and scatter over the citrus.

3. In a small bowl, stir together maple syrup and cinnamon. Drizzle the spiced syrup all over the fruit. Garnish with a sprinkling of salt and serve at once.

TIP: *Save time in the morning by doing some prep ahead. The evening before your breakfast or brunch, remove the peel from all the citrus, but do not slice the fruit. Stash the citrus in an airtight container, cover and refrigerate until ready to use. In the morning, simply unwrap the fruit and proceed from step 2.*

Roasted Apple and Ginger Tisane

SERVES 2 · REQUIRES TIME FOR PREP

This autumnal tea is all about clean flavours and natural ingredients. With the first pour, its fragrant vapours wrap you in a warm hug. The honey and ginger soothe the throat, and the apple infusion is pronounced yet subtle. I tend to save bruised and battered, old and wrinkled apples for this tea. Once they are roasted, they taste just as good as young, unblemished apples.

To customize the flavours, slip a sprig of thyme or rosemary in place of the ginger or add a drop of vanilla. Of course, you can always just enjoy the apple tisane on its own.

3 medium apples, such as Cortland or McIntosh

½-inch (1 cm) slice fresh ginger

Liquid honey, for serving

Apple slice, for garnish

1. Preheat oven to 350°F (180°C).

2. Wash apples well, then cut them in half and place them in a small baking pan. Roast apples for about 45 minutes, until their skins begin to wrinkle and the juices begin to seep out. Meanwhile, boil a kettle of water.

3. Cut each apple half in two and place them in a clean 1-quart (1 L) mason jar. If any apple juice accumulated in the pan, tip it into the jar as well. Add the slice of ginger and fill the jar with just-boiled water. Cover with a lid and let tisane steep in a warm place for about an hour.

4. Strain tea into a cup and sweeten with honey to taste. You may want to gently reheat the tisane, as it will have cooled considerably. Float an apple slice on top, then find a quiet place to savour your cup. The tisane will keep, refrigerated in the jar, for up to 3 days before it loses its fresh taste.

Wholesome Lunches and Snacks

With two kids in elementary school and a spouse who takes a lunch to work every day, I'm familiar with the ups and downs of packing a bagged lunch. I know it gets old, that certain foods become routine all too often, and that your efforts can go unappreciated. I also know that folks are short on time and that it's a big help to make lunch box foods ahead. Fresh and nourishing lunches take a bit of planning, but are worth the extra effort.

It is with all this in mind that I have assembled a collection of my best snack and lunch ideas for both kids and adults.

Things haven't always been hunky-dory in the school lunch department. When my children first started school, I learned a vital lesson in nutrition, communication and, well, parenting. The boys would frequently come home irritable, falling apart at the slightest grievance, snappy and unable to focus. I'd power through those tough afternoons, assuming they were just tired or out of sorts. I'd tidy up their lunch boxes, so distracted that I hardly noticed what was left in them.

Eventually, I connected the dots. On the difficult days, there was a lot of leftover food in their lunch boxes. Perhaps they had wasted time during their lunch hour or disliked what I had packed for them, but whatever the reason, their energy wasn't sustained for the whole day. We started talking more about their preferences (how fortunate we are to have options!). We made lunch boxes together in the morning and built a midday meal they couldn't wait to eat. Together we learned even more about seasonal eating, and they picked out their favourite fruits and vegetables for each month. On weekends we baked together and made Whole Wheat Chocolate Zucchini Bread (page 91), Pepper Parmesan Crackers (page 98) and Lemon Cornmeal Madeleines (page 92), then froze the goodies for future lunches. Fortunately, things turned around, and those crotchety after-school attitudes are now a thing of the past.

One of my daily goals is to make lunches as nourishing as possible while providing foods my kids will realistically eat. Moderation plays a big part in finding this balance. We aim for a mainly homemade lunch, but processed snacks do make an occasional appearance. For example, when they bemoaned the fact that simply *everybody* else had juice boxes every day, we instigated "Juicebox Friday": once a week they get an (unsweetened!) box of juice in their lunch, a happy compromise.

As the years go by, I continue to learn about the lunch box. For example, as my boys are getting older, I realized that bigger kids need a bigger thermos. Skip the cute lunch box for tweens and teens and invest in a good, and good-sized, thermos for packing leftovers, soups and stews. And it's worth mentioning that kids' appetites vary widely. One boy eats far more than his brother and empties his lunch box every day. I know to pack a few extra items for him—and then be understanding when he's not as hungry for dinner.

I also quickly discovered that the lunch box is not the place to try new foods. School lunches should be a familiar taste of home. It is best to introduce new dishes at home, where you can talk about them and collect feedback from your children. Remember, kids don't crave variety in their diet like we do. Don't be worried if they want the same thing day in and day out for weeks on end.

By the time this book is published, my youngest, Clara, will be just starting kindergarten, and another twelve years of school lunches are in store for us. Here's to facing the future together, one lunch box at a time.

LUNCH BOX RENEWAL

How do you liven up the doldrums of the daily bagged lunch? I have a few ideas to share, gathered from years of packing lunches for both work and school.

BAKE IT Home-baked goods can be made in advance, frozen and brought out a few at a time. Honey Whole Wheat Bagels (page 39) and Whole Wheat Pita Bread (page 68) instantly become the star of any lunch box they are added to, especially when paired with Gin-Cured Gravlax (page 151), Classic Greek Tzatziki (page 147)— or both. Beef Empanadas (page 83) are a treat, paired with mustard and a salad on the side. And don't forget about my homemade Pepper Parmesan Crackers (page 98); I like to get the kids involved with rolling and cutting and bake a few batches to freeze for the start of the school year. Then I pack them with sliced cheese and pepperoni for an irresistible snack.

BUILD A BOWL (OR A JAR) Generous, nutritious salad bowls are all the rage these days. Essentially you are removing the carbs from a popular dish and piling it on greens instead. Sushi bowls, fajita bowls, taco bowls—all you need to do is combine your favourite proteins and vegetables in a bowl or a wide-mouth mason jar and pack a dressing on the side. Try the Tangy Quinoa Carrot Chicken Salad (page 75) to get on board with this trend.

SLURP A SMOOTHIE A generous smoothie, packed with both vegetables and fruits and thinned out with a nut milk, makes a healthy and satisfying lunch. Avocado, pumpkin purée, grated fresh carrot, spinach, roasted sweet potato, grated fresh beet—these are all vegetables I regularly add to my smoothies. Add some zip to your creations with a grating of ginger or turmeric—and don't forget to pack a straw. My Blushing Apple, Beet and Cherry Smoothie (page 52) is a great recipe to start with.

Another good idea is to make smoothies ahead of time and store them in the freezer in plastic freezer-jam containers. By lunchtime, they're soft enough to enjoy, and they help keep any other perishable foods in the lunch box cool.

DOUBLE UP ON DINNER I'm a big proponent of reworking leftovers into a hearty lunch. Be they Baked Buttermilk Chicken Strips (page 81), cold roast beef for sandwiching with Green Olive Tapenade (page 76) or Whole Simmered Chicken (page 213), leftovers are the best building blocks for a hearty lunch. Plan a few make-ahead meals and freeze them in individual portions. I do this with my Mild Chicken and Chickpea Curry (page 205) as well as Slow Cooker Root Vegetable Cider Stew (page 131). My future self is always thankful.

WRAP WONDERS I always have several packs of whole wheat wraps in my freezer. Wraps need not be more complicated than tortilla + leftovers + condiments. Last night's roast chicken with a little mayonnaise and lettuce is wrap-worthy, as is Tofu Vegetable Stir-Fry with Cashews (page 121) with a scrambled egg. We all love the Roasted Sweet Potato, Pesto and Bacon Wrap (page 78).

SOUP SEASON Don't be daunted by potential transportation issues; invest in a good thermos and pack a soup at least once a week. I like to make a double batch, then freeze it in individual portions. I thaw them the evening before, then reheat in the morning. Roasted Tomato and Lentil Soup (page 118) is my favourite, paired with Herbed Croutons (page 159).

HEALTHY SWEETS Pack an afternoon treat that won't leave anyone crashing after a sugar high. A thick slice of Whole Wheat Chocolate Chunk Zucchini Bread (page 91) or a Tahini Maple Tea Cookie (page 97) are both treats that will satisfy a craving but won't wind you or the kids up on sugar.

LUNCH BOX REVITALIZERS Try adding a few of these foods to your shopping list or make your own. Then incorporate these lunch box revitalizers into your usual lunch in the most creative way possible.

- Sprouts and microgreens—great on sandwiches and in salads, or even as a crunchy topping to soup.
- Baby arugula or spinach—heap on leftover pizza or grain salads or toss into wraps and sandwiches.
- Pickles—pile them on virtually anything for extra crunch and welcome tang.
- Bold sheep or goat cheese—delicious on salads, grain dishes and pastas.
- Fresh herbs—use with abandon, tearing them and adding to the dish just before you eat.
- Toasted nuts and seeds—toast in small batches and use up in a few days.
- Ferments—kimchi, Simple Sauerkraut (page 268) or other ferments add an exciting element to lunches.

Super-Seed Yogurt Parfait

Some of the best super-seeds join forces in this easily portable lunch. Chia, sesame, sunflower and nutty hulled pumpkin seeds get tossed together with a dusting of wheat germ, hemp hearts and ground flaxseed for a potpourri of power foods. Scoop this mix over yogurt with fresh pomegranate and a drizzle of honey and I guarantee that this nourishing jar will keep you going until dinnertime.

This parfait can double as a desk breakfast or lunch, depending on how soon hunger strikes in your day. Make the toasted mix of seeds ahead of time and store in an airtight container at room temperature for up to 1 week, or longer in the freezer. Having the mix premade means you can get out the door with your parfait even faster. Hurray!

2 tablespoons (30 mL) raw pepitas

1 tablespoon (15 mL) sesame seeds

1 tablespoon (15 mL) raw sunflower seeds

1 tablespoon (15 mL) chia seeds

1 tablespoon (15 mL) hemp hearts

1 tablespoon (15 mL) wheat germ

1 tablespoon (15 mL) ground flaxseed

1 cup (250 mL) pomegranate seeds

1 cup (250 mL) full-fat plain organic yogurt

2 teaspoons (10 mL) liquid honey or pure maple syrup

1. Preheat oven to 325°F (160°C).

2. Combine pepitas, sesame seeds, sunflower seeds, chia seeds, hemp hearts, wheat germ and flaxseed on a small rimmed baking sheet lined with parchment paper. Toast in the oven for 7 to 8 minutes. The wheat germ will begin to smell toasty. Cool completely.

3. Spoon a few tablespoons of yogurt into two 1-cup (250 mL) jars. Divide most of the pomegranate seeds between the jars. Add a heaping spoonful of toasted seeds to each jar.

4. Divide remaining yogurt and seeds between the jars. Sprinkle with remaining pomegranate seeds. Finish each parfait with 1 teaspoon (5 mL) of honey drizzled over each. Enjoy at once or cover with a lid and refrigerate for up to 6 hours.

Whole Wheat Pita Bread

MAKES 8 (6-INCH/15 CM) PUFFED PITAS · REQUIRES TIME FOR PREP

The best school days are when I can stuff a homemade pita with a little roast chicken, lettuce and tzatziki and pack it in the boys' lunches along with fresh cucumbers and olives. Pitas are one of my preferred jump-starts for my own weekday lunches as well, stuffed with Tangy Quinoa Carrot Chicken Salad (page 75) or vegetables and boiled eggs in my Turkish Breakfast Pita (page 71). Pitas are for more than the lunch box, though. Cut them into wedges while still warm and serve them alongside a bowl of hummus or Classic Greek Tzatziki (page 147).

1 tablespoon (15 mL) active dry yeast

1 cup (250 mL) wrist-warm water (105 to 115°F/38 to 40°C)

¼ cup (60 mL) Homemade Buttermilk (page 228) or store-bought

1½ teaspoons (7 mL) fine sea salt

2½ cups (625 mL) whole wheat bread flour

1. In the bowl of a stand mixer fitted with the dough hook, sprinkle the yeast over the warm water. Stir with a fork to help the yeast activate, then let bloom for 5 minutes.

2. Add Homemade Buttermilk, salt and 1½ cups (375 mL) of the flour. Beat on medium speed to make a batter. Scrape down the sides of the bowl. Add the remaining 1 cup (250 mL) flour and mix on low speed until a rough, shaggy mass forms and the dough comes together. Turn off mixer and let the dough rest for 10 minutes to give the liquid a chance to soften the bran and the germ in the flour.

3. Knead the dough on low speed for 8 minutes, or until it is smooth and elastic. It will be quite soft. Add a little more flour if it is too sticky.

4. Turn dough out onto a lightly floured counter and divide it into 8 pieces. Don't worry if they are not exactly the same size. Form each piece into a ball, loosely rolling it in a circular motion under the palm of your hand.

5. With a lightly floured rolling pin, roll each ball into a 6- or 7-inch (15 or 18 cm) round about ⅛ inch (3 mm) thick. Try to keep them an even thickness, as this is what helps them puff. I like to alternate rolling with the rolling pin pointed "east and west" and then "north and south."

6. Line two baking sheets with parchment paper. Delicately place 4 rounds of dough on each baking sheet. Cover loosely with clean tea towels and let rest for 45 minutes until slightly puffed. Meanwhile, preheat oven to 475°F (240°C) and position oven racks in the upper and lower thirds of the oven.

7. Bake pitas for 8 to 9 minutes without opening the oven door. Stick around to watch them puff around the 4-minute mark. Pitas will puff and turn a light golden, but still be soft and flexible. If you prefer a pita with slightly crispy edges, bake for an additional 2 to 3 minutes.

8. Cool pitas on a wire rack. Pitas are best enjoyed the day they are made, but leftovers can be sealed in a freezer bag and frozen for up to 8 weeks.

Turkish Breakfast Pita

SERVES 2

When I was nineteen, I hitchhiked through Turkey for two weeks as part of a greater trip across Mediterranean Europe. I travelled from Istanbul out to Cappadocia, then down to Antalya and up to the ancient city of Ephesus, nearly bursting from eating in every place. While I hold dear the memories of pide, börek, köfte and more, after all these years it is the simple Turkish breakfast that I re-create the most often in my own kitchen.

The ingredients below are traditionally arranged on a plate and served with a side of honey, but for the portable desk lunch, I like to stuff everything into a homemade pita. My Whole Wheat Pita Bread (page 68) holds up well to the task. Enjoy this breakfast-for-lunch with a cup of steaming Roasted Apple and Ginger Tisane (page 56) and imagine yourself in one of the fairy chimneys of the Anatolian plains.

1 English cucumber

1 large tomato

¼ teaspoon (1 mL) sea salt

2 Whole Wheat Pita Breads (page 68), halved

2 tablespoons (30 mL) salted butter, softened

2 hard-boiled eggs

¼ cup (60 mL) Kalamata olives, pitted

⅛ small red onion, sliced

2 ounces (55 g) feta cheese, crumbled

2 tablespoons (30 mL) torn fresh flat-leaf parsley

1. Peel and slice the cucumber. Core, halve and slice the tomato into wedges. Season cucumber and tomato with salt. Gently open the pita halves and spread with butter.

2. Wedge the pita halves upright in a bowl or other container (I like to use a loaf pan). Stuff pitas with cucumber and tomato. Slice the eggs and add to the pitas along with the olives and red onion. Sprinkle with feta and finish with a generous helping of fresh parsley.

3. Enjoy right away or pack into an airtight container and refrigerate. These are best enjoyed within about 3 hours.

Farro, Feta and Tomato Salad with Red Onion Vinaigrette

SERVES 4

I've gotten into the habit of keeping a bowl of cooked farro or quinoa in the refrigerator so my lunches come together with minimal effort. Farro is a versatile ancient grain with a nutty flavour that pairs well with delicate tomatoes and mild herbs. Its delightfully chewy texture holds up well to bold vinaigrettes, and this salad doesn't get soggy after an overnight stay in the refrigerator. If you can, make the vinaigrette the day before to let the flavours mellow. You can cook the farro in advance, too. If Romanesco cauliflower is out of season, use diced celery or fennel instead.

Red onion vinaigrette

¼ cup (60 mL) minced red onion

¼ cup (60 mL) extra-virgin olive oil

2 tablespoons (30 mL) red wine vinegar

1 teaspoon (5 mL) Dijon mustard

½ teaspoon (2 mL) sea salt

Farro, feta and tomato salad

¾ cup (175 mL) farro

2½ cups (625 mL) water

1 pint (500 mL) sweet cherry tomatoes, halved

1 cup (250 mL) coarsely chopped Romanesco cauliflower

½ cup (125 mL) crumbled feta

¼ cup (60 mL) raw pepitas

1 small bunch flat-leaf parsley, finely chopped

1. **MAKE THE RED ONION VINAIGRETTE** In a small jar, combine the onion, olive oil, red wine vinegar, mustard and salt. Cover with a lid and shake well to mix.

2. **MAKE THE FARRO, FETA AND TOMATO SALAD** Rinse farro under cool running water; drain and add to a medium saucepan. Add the water and salt to taste. Cover and bring to a boil over high heat. Reduce heat to low and simmer, covered, for 25 to 30 minutes, or until farro is tender yet still chewy. Remove from heat, drain off any excess water and cool completely.

3. In a large bowl, combine cooled farro, tomatoes, Romanesco, feta, pepitas and parsley. Mix well. Pour the vinaigrette over the farro salad and mix well again. Add salt to taste. Serve at once or refrigerate in an airtight container for up to 2 days.

Tangy Quinoa Carrot Chicken Salad

SERVES 2

I like my lunchtime salads with a little heat, a dash of spice and plenty of crunch. This recipe has it all, an antidote to mid-winter blahs. I use leftover roast chicken or my Whole Simmered Chicken (page 213) for a boost of protein in the salad, but for a vegetarian version, it's also delicious with black beans.

If you can't find fresh cilantro, or can't eat it, use peppery watercress or arugula in its place. If Meyer lemons are in season, replace the lime with one and chop up a little of the pulp to add to the vinaigrette.

½ cup (125 mL) red quinoa

1 cup (250 mL) water

1 small clove garlic, minced

1 tablespoon (15 mL) rice vinegar

Zest and juice of 1 lime

¾ teaspoon (4 mL) fine sea salt

½ teaspoon (2 mL) crushed coriander seeds

¼ teaspoon (1 mL) ground cumin

2 tablespoons (30 mL) extra-virgin olive oil

4 medium carrots, peeled and grated (about 2 cups/500 mL)

1 jalapeño pepper, seeded and thinly sliced

2 cups (500 mL) shredded cooked chicken

1 medium bunch cilantro

1. Combine the quinoa and the water in a medium saucepan. Cover and bring to a boil over high heat. Reduce heat to medium-low and cook for 12 minutes, until fluffy and tender. Cool completely.

2. Meanwhile, make the dressing. In a small bowl, stir together the garlic and rice vinegar. Add the lime zest and juice, salt, coriander and cumin. Slowly whisk in olive oil until creamy.

3. In a large bowl, toss together carrots, jalapeño, chicken and quinoa. Pour over the vinaigrette and mix well. Roughly chop the cilantro and toss into the salad. Serve immediately.

TIP: *If you'd like to make this as a layered salad in a mason jar, follow this order: dressing first, then quinoa, chicken, carrots, jalapeño and lastly cilantro.*

Green Olive Tapenade

MAKES 1 CUP (250 ML)

✤

Here's a lunch box condiment that will awaken the taste buds. We like to slather this bright and citrusy sandwich spread on Whole Wheat Pita Bread (page 68), pair it with crackers and cheese or occasionally dollop it onto Egg-Topped Umami Oatmeal (page 47). My favourite sandwich features this tapenade on crusty whole wheat bread with cold roast beef, alfalfa sprouts and thick slices of sweet white onion.

This recipe might include ingredients that are new to you, but they all keep well in the refrigerator for some time, so the investment is worthwhile. Besides, once you begin incorporating this tapenade into lunches, you'll wonder how you ever lived without a jar of it in your refrigerator.

1 cup (250 mL) green olives, pitted

1 large clove garlic, peeled

2 tablespoons (30 mL) flat-leaf parsley leaves

2 teaspoons (10 mL) fresh thyme leaves

1 tablespoon (15 mL) chopped Preserved Meyer Lemons with Bay Leaf (page 263) or store-bought preserved lemon

1 tablespoon (15 mL) capers, rinsed

1 tablespoon (15 mL) freshly squeezed lemon juice

½ teaspoon (2 mL) prepared horseradish

¼ teaspoon (1 mL) anchovy paste

½ cup (125 mL) extra-virgin olive oil

1. In a food processor, combine the olives, garlic, parsley, thyme, Preserved Meyer Lemons, capers, lemon juice, horseradish and anchovy paste. Process for several seconds, then stop the machine and scrape down the sides. Repeat several times, pulverizing and scraping, until the ingredients are finely ground and no longer individually distinguishable.

2. With the machine running, drizzle in the olive oil. The tapenade will be a thick, fragrant green paste. Transfer to a jar, cover and refrigerate overnight for the flavours to develop. You can store the tapenade, refrigerated in the jar, for up to 3 weeks.

Roasted Sweet Potato, Pesto and Bacon Wrap

※

Nourishing and simple to make, these are among our favourite lunch or breakfast-on-the-go wraps. They are endlessly versatile—leave out the bacon and double up on the spinach for a vegetarian version; add scrambled eggs for a breakfast wrap; include sliced avocado for a little creaminess; or swap out the pesto for Green Olive Tapenade (page 76) for a bright burst of flavour.

If you have a little bacon grease left over, toss the sweet potatoes in that in place of the olive oil. If you're not cooking for children, add a dash of cayenne in addition to the paprika.

1 medium sweet potato, peeled

1 teaspoon (5 mL) extra-virgin olive oil

¼ teaspoon (1 mL) sweet or hot smoked paprika

¼ teaspoon (1 mL) sea salt

¼ teaspoon (1 mL) freshly ground black pepper

2 tablespoons (30 mL) Basil and Pepita Pesto (page 247)

2 whole wheat wraps

2 handfuls baby spinach

2 slices thick-cut bacon, cooked

1. Preheat oven to 425°F (220°C).

2. Cut sweet potato in half lengthwise, then cut each half into 4 wedges. Toss wedges with olive oil, paprika, salt and pepper. Arrange in a single layer on a rimmed baking sheet and roast for 20 to 25 minutes, turning at least once, until light brown on the outside and soft on the inside. Cool completely.

3. Spread Basil and Pepita Pesto over the wraps, then divide the spinach between the two. Arrange 4 roasted sweet potato wedges on each wrap and top with a slice of bacon.

4. Roll wrap tightly and then wrap in wax paper. Slice on the diagonal and enjoy right away or keep refrigerated until ready for lunch.

Baked Buttermilk Chicken Strips

A Worcestershire-spiked buttermilk marinade and a brown-butter crispy topping make these chicken strips irresistible to both kids and adults alike. They are delicious crisped in the oven and then wrapped in foil or tucked into a heated bento box for school lunch. We also love these for dinner and frequently make a double batch, putting away half for the next day's lunches. The kids help with the breading to speed things along.

Note that the chicken strips require time to marinate. Be sure to build that into your schedule.

2 boneless, skinless chicken breasts

¾ cup (175 mL) Homemade Buttermilk (page 228) or store-bought

1¼ teaspoons (6 mL) Worcestershire sauce, divided

¾ teaspoon (3 mL) sea salt, divided

¾ teaspoon (3 mL) freshly ground black pepper, divided

½ teaspoon (2 mL) sweet smoked paprika

2 tablespoons (30 mL) unsalted butter

1 cup (250 mL) panko crumbs

2 large eggs

½ cup (125 mL) all-purpose flour

Mustard or liquid honey, for dipping

1. Using a chef's knife, cut the chicken breasts into "fingers," about 5 per breast. Tap the thicker parts with the side of the knife to even out the thickness. They should be about ½ inch (1 cm) thick at most.

2. In a medium-size container with a lid, combine Homemade Buttermilk, 1 teaspoon (5 mL) of the Worcestershire sauce, ½ teaspoon (2 mL) of the salt, ½ teaspoon (2 mL) of the pepper and the paprika; stir well. Add the chicken strips and turn to coat. Cover the container tightly and refrigerate the chicken for at least 6 hours or overnight.

3. Position an oven rack in the upper third of the oven and preheat oven to 375°F (190°C). Lightly brush a wire rack with oil and place it on a rimmed baking sheet.

4. In a small saucepan, melt butter gently over medium heat. Keep a close eye on it as it foams and changes to a light golden colour. It will smell slightly nutty. Be careful not to let it burn. Remove the browned butter from heat.

(recipe continues)

5. Combine panko and browned butter in a small bowl and stir well to coat the crumbs. Transfer to a pie plate or shallow bowl. In another bowl, beat the eggs with the remaining ¼ teaspoon (1 mL) Worcestershire sauce. In a third bowl, combine the flour with the remaining ¼ teaspoon (1 mL) salt and remaining ¼ teaspoon (1 mL) pepper.

6. Drain the chicken, discarding the Homemade Buttermilk. Using tongs and working with one strip of chicken at a time, dredge chicken through the flour to coat, then the egg, and lastly the buttery panko. Place the crumb-coated chicken on the prepared rack. Repeat with the remaining chicken, allowing at least 1 inch (2.5 cm) of space around each chicken strip.

7. Bake for 18 to 20 minutes or until the panko is pale golden and the chicken is cooked through. Finish under the broiler for an extra-crispy, dark brown coating. Serve hot with a dollop of mustard or a drizzle of honey.

TIP: *The cooked chicken fingers freeze well. Reheat from frozen for 20 to 25 minutes at 350°F (180°C) on the middle oven rack.*

Beef Empanadas

MAKES 36 EMPANADAS · REQUIRES TIME FOR PREP

I have my Peruvian friend Elizabeth to thank for this empanada recipe. She delivered a box of them shortly after I had Clara, and we all became instant fans of the popular meat pie. Of course I had to learn how to make them, and so my education took place in Liz's beautiful kitchen under her patient tutelage.

Empanadas are a near-perfect homemade convenience food. They transport well, are easy to eat and are very filling—ideal lunch box material, if you ask me. We adore the traditional filling of ground beef, hard-boiled eggs, olives, onions and seasonings (we tend to leave out the raisins), but empanadas can be as versatile as you like. Try them stuffed with chicken and green olives, spiced pork and potatoes, braised lentils, or even apples for a dessert variety.

Break up the work by prepping the dough and the filling, chilling both overnight and assembling the empanadas the next day. The kids and I have fun rolling and cutting the dough, but if you're short on time you can buy rounds of empanada dough at specialty grocery stores. Many hands make light work, and we all pitch in on a big batch and freeze the extras for school lunches.

Dough

3 cups (750 mL) all-purpose flour

1 cup (250 mL) whole wheat flour

1 tablespoon (15 mL) raw cane sugar

½ teaspoon (2 mL) sea salt

1¼ cups (300 mL) cold unsalted butter

¾ cup (175 mL) water

1 tablespoon (15 mL) white vinegar

2 eggs, beaten with 1 teaspoon (5 mL) water, for egg wash

Beef filling

3 tablespoons (45 mL) extra-virgin olive oil

2 medium red onions, chopped

2 large white onions, chopped

2 medium cloves garlic, minced

2 pounds (900 g) lean ground beef

2 large tomatoes, chopped

1 teaspoon (5 mL) fine sea salt

½ teaspoon (2 mL) freshly ground black pepper

1 bunch green onions, finely chopped

Additional fillings

2 hard-boiled eggs, chopped

¼ cup (60 mL) Kalamata olives, pitted and chopped

1. **MAKE THE DOUGH** In the bowl of a stand mixer, combine the all-purpose flour, whole wheat flour, sugar and salt. Using the large holes of a box grater, grate the cold butter into the flour, then toss with the flour to coat. Attach the paddle hook and mix on low speed for 1 minute to blend the butter into the flour.

(recipe continues)

2.   Stir together the water and vinegar. With the mixer on low speed, add the water and vinegar mixture to the flour a few teaspoons at a time, until the dough comes together in a shaggy mass. Stop the mixer. Gather the dough together, divide in half and shape each into a ball. Wrap each ball in plastic wrap. Chill for at least 2 hours and up to overnight.

3.   **MAKE THE BEEF FILLING** Heat olive oil in your largest heavy pot over medium-low heat. Add the red and white onions and cook until the onions are soft, about 10 minutes, stirring occasionally.

4.   Add the garlic and beef and break the meat into small mince using a wooden spoon. Increase heat to medium and brown the beef with the onions for an additional 10 minutes, stirring frequently.

5.   Tumble in the chopped tomatoes, salt and pepper; stir the filling very well. Cook for 30 to 40 minutes, until the tomatoes have cooked down and the liquid has evaporated. Turn off heat and stir in green onions. Spread the mixture on a rimmed baking sheet to cool completely. Refrigerate if you have space.

6.   **ASSEMBLE THE EMPANADAS** Preheat oven to 350°F (180°C).

7.   Roll out one ball of the dough to 1/16-inch (2 mm) thickness. Using a 4½-inch (11 cm) round cookie cutter, cut out 18 to 20 circles. (You may find it easier to pinch off golf ball–size pieces of dough and roll them individually.) Place a generous tablespoon of filling in the centre of each dough disc. Top with a small piece each of hard-boiled egg and olive. Brush the edges with the egg wash. Fold one edge over the other, keeping the filling tucked into the centre, and press the edges together to form a half moon. You can seal the edges by pressing them with a fork, or you can make a traditional empanada twist by folding the edges over and crimping in place (this takes practice!).

8.   Place empanadas on a baking sheet, about an inch (2.5 cm) apart. Brush with egg wash. Bake for about 40 minutes, until deep golden brown. Repeat with remaining ball of dough and filling. Also re-roll any scraps of dough and fill. Enjoy baked empanadas hot and cool the remainder on a wire rack.

> TIP: *You can freeze the empanadas before baking them. Place them on a baking sheet without touching each other and freeze until solid. Transfer to freezer bags and freeze for up to 1 year. To cook, place frozen empanadas on a baking sheet and brush with egg wash. Bake at 350°F (180°C) until golden brown, about 50 minutes.*

Sauerkraut and Swiss Grilled Cheese Sandwiches

SERVES 2

∞

I've had a long obsession with sauerkraut that has spurned many strange creations, but this hearty grilled cheese is one of my best ideas. It's a winter lunchtime staple, satisfying those cravings for all things crunchy, tangy and cheesy. For an exceptional lunch, serve with a side of Baby Dill Pickles (page 270) and a round of Bloody Caesars (page 166).

You won't miss the meat in this satisfying sandwich, but I won't judge should you slip in a few slices of Montreal smoked meat.

1 cup (250 mL) Simple Sauerkraut (page 268)

4 large slices rustic caraway rye bread

2 teaspoons (10 mL) grainy mustard, or to taste

8 slices Swiss or Emmental cheese

2 to 3 tablespoons (30 to 45 mL) salted butter, softened

1. Heat a large cast-iron skillet over medium heat.

2. Drain Simple Sauerkraut and pat dry with paper towels. Arrange the bread on a cutting board and spread one side of bread slices with mustard.

3. Place 2 slices of cheese on 2 slices of bread. Heap the drained Simple Sauerkraut on the cheese. Top with the remaining cheese, followed by the remaining bread.

4. Spread butter on the outsides of both sandwiches. Place them in the hot pan and reduce heat to medium-low. Place a pie plate on top of the sandwiches and weigh it down with a tea kettle or another heavy pan.

5. Toast sandwiches for 4 to 5 minutes, until the bottom is golden brown. Turn and cook on the other side for an additional 2 to 3 minutes, until the bread is toasted and the cheese is melted.

6. Slice sandwiches in half and serve at once.

Josh's Borscht

SERVES 6 TO 8

My siblings and I all make our versions of the traditional Ukrainian soup that my mother grew up eating. My brother Josh always surprises me with the love and care that he puts into his borscht; of course that is probably precisely why his recipe is the best. Josh will protest that his borscht isn't very traditional because it includes so many vegetables, but we can overlook custom and celebrate the local harvest instead.

For a vegetarian version, leave out the kielbasa and use Basic Vegetable Stock (page 231). I keep a box of latex gloves in the kitchen for when I'm working with beets (and doing other messy jobs).

2 large red beets

2 medium carrots

1 medium red-skinned potato

1 medium onion

3 stalks celery

1 tablespoon (15 mL) extra-virgin olive oil or bacon fat

5 ounces (140 g) kielbasa or ham sausage, diced

6 cups (1.5 L) beef stock or Basic Vegetable Stock (page 231)

1 small zucchini, diced

1 cup (250 mL) finely chopped Brussels sprouts

2 cups (500 mL) shredded red cabbage

2 cups (500 mL) chopped beet greens (optional)

2 tablespoons (30 mL) chopped fresh dill

2 tablespoons (30 mL) white vinegar

Salt and freshly ground black pepper

Full-fat plain organic yogurt or sour cream, for topping

1. Begin by prepping your root vegetables. Peel the beets, carrots and potato and dice everything up. It's best if the beets are a slightly smaller dice than the other vegetables, as they take a little longer to cook. Dice the onion and the celery, too, but keep them separate from the root vegtables.

2. Heat the olive oil in a large pot over medium-high heat. Add the kielbasa and sauté, stirring often, for about 2 minutes. Add the onion and celery and cook alongside the sausage for a few more minutes, until the onions soften.

3. Tumble in the beets, carrots and potato. Pour in the beef stock and bring to a boil. Reduce heat and simmer until root vegetables are al dente, about 10 minutes.

4. Stir in the zucchini, Brussels sprouts, cabbage and beet greens, if using. Return to a boil, then reduce heat and simmer the soup for 10 minutes or until the vegetables are tender. Sprinkle in the dill and the vinegar. Season the borscht to taste with salt and pepper. Ladle into bowls and serve with a dollop of yogurt or sour cream.

5. Cool completely before refrigerating the leftovers in airtight containers. Borscht will keep for up to 5 days in the fridge and up to 6 months in the freezer.

Whole Wheat Chocolate Chunk Zucchini Bread

The most basic zucchini bread is a treat in itself, but when it is enhanced with a hint of spice and studded with dark chocolate, it becomes truly special. This loaf is utterly delicious with the chopped walnuts, although I keep my version nut-free so the kids can take a slab in their lunch box.

This bread is even better on the second day; keep it at room temperature well wrapped in plastic—and try to hide it from the kids.

1½ cups (375 mL) whole wheat flour

1 cup (250 mL) all-purpose flour

1 teaspoon (5 mL) baking powder

½ teaspoon (2 mL) baking soda

½ teaspoon (2 mL) fine sea salt

1 tablespoon (15 mL) ground cinnamon

¼ teaspoon (1 mL) freshly grated nutmeg

½ cup (125 mL) unsalted butter, at room temperature

1 cup (250 mL) raw cane sugar

2 medium eggs, at room temperature

½ cup (125 mL) full-fat plain organic yogurt

1 teaspoon (5 mL) pure vanilla extract

2 cups (500 mL) grated zucchini, drained (about 10 ounces/280 g whole zucchini)

¼ cup (60 mL) Homemade Buttermilk (page 228) or store-bought

¾ cup (175 mL) roughly chopped dark chocolate

1. Preheat oven to 325°F (160°C). Oil a 9- × 5-inch (2 L) loaf pan and line the bottom and sides with parchment paper.

2. In a medium bowl, sift together whole wheat flour, all-purpose flour, baking powder, baking soda, salt, cinnamon and nutmeg.

3. In a large bowl, beat the butter and sugar until creamy. Beat in the eggs one at a time, then add the yogurt and vanilla and beat well. With a large spatula, stir in the grated zucchini.

4. Fold flour mixture into the wet ingredients, along with the Homemade Buttermilk, until combined, being careful not to overmix. Fold in the chopped chocolate.

5. Scrape batter into the loaf pan. Bake for 70 to 80 minutes, until the middle is set but still springy and a toothpick inserted in the centre comes out with just a few crumbs attached. Cool in the pan for 10 minutes. Loosen the sides and remove loaf from pan. Cool completely on a wire rack before slicing. The loaf keeps well, wrapped in plastic wrap, for up to 4 days.

Lemon Cornmeal Madeleines

MAKES 18 MADELEINES · REQUIRES TIME FOR PREP

My son Noah's absolute favourite treat is a fresh-baked madeleine—or three—so I developed a nut-free version that I could send in his lunch box. The batter chills overnight, and I bake them up fresh on school mornings.

For unforgettable flavour, use Meyer lemons when they are in season. Note that the recipe uses the zest, so zest your lemons *before* juicing them.

3 medium eggs

½ cup (125 mL) raw cane sugar

¼ teaspoon (1 mL) fine sea salt

Zest of 2 lemons

3 tablespoons (45 mL) freshly squeezed lemon juice

1 cup (250 mL) all-purpose flour

1 teaspoon (5 mL) baking powder

¼ cup (60 mL) fine cornmeal

½ teaspoon (2 mL) ground cardamom

½ cup (125 mL) unsalted butter, melted and cooled, plus more for pans

1. In a large bowl, whisk together the eggs, sugar and salt until frothy. Whisk in lemon zest and juice.

2. In another bowl, sift together flour and baking powder. Whisk in cornmeal and cardamom.

3. Fold dry ingredients into the wet. Pour the melted butter over the batter and fold to just combine. Cover and chill batter overnight or for at least 6 hours.

4. Preheat oven to 400°F (200°C). Generously brush melted butter into the moulds of a madeleine pan, being sure to cover every crease. Lightly dust with all-purpose flour and then tap the pan upside down over the sink to remove excess flour.

5. Scoop a heaping tablespoon (20 mL) of batter into each mould. Bake for 13 to 15 minutes, until the tops puff and the edges are slightly browned. Immediately invert the pan over a wire rack and tap gently to dislodge the madeleines.

6. Wash the pan, cool completely, then butter and flour it again and bake the remaining batter. Cool madeleines completely on a wire rack before packing up for lunches. Store in an airtight container at room temperature for up to 3 days. Madeleines can be frozen for up to 3 months.

Granola Cluster Trail Mix

MAKES 4 CUPS (1 L)

My children's love of granola knows no bounds—so much so that I had to create this lunch box snack as an excuse to let them eat it at lunch as well as breakfast. This addicting trail mix replaces the processed granola bar in the school lunch and works for snacking on the go. The clusters are packed with goodness such as hemp hearts and seeds to give maximum energy. Pumpkin purée acts as a binder and just feels natural when the kids are heading back to school in the fall.

Once you make the granola clusters, feel free to customize your trail mix as you like: dried apricots and white chocolate chips; dried goji berries and dark chocolate. I've left out nuts, since most schools won't allow them, but if this is intended for your desk lunch or the children at home, add a big handful of cashews, almonds or your favourite snacking nut.

2 tablespoons (30 mL) pure pumpkin purée or unsweetened applesauce

2 tablespoons (30 mL) pure maple syrup

1 tablespoon (15 mL) extra-virgin olive oil

¼ teaspoon (1 mL) Autumn Spice Blend (page 244)

1 cup (250 mL) old-fashioned rolled oats

2 tablespoons (30 mL) hemp hearts

2 tablespoons (30 mL) raw sunflower seeds

1 small egg white

Pinch of sea salt

Optional add-ins

¼ cup (60 mL) raw pepitas

¼ cup (60 mL) dark chocolate chunks

¼ cup (60 mL) unsweetened dried cherries

¼ cup (60 mL) golden raisins

¼ cup (60 mL) unsweetened flaked coconut

1. Preheat oven to 300°F (150°C). Line a rimmed baking sheet with parchment paper.

2. In a medium bowl, stir together pumpkin purée, maple syrup, olive oil and Autumn Spice Blend. Tumble in rolled oats, hemp hearts and sunflower seeds; toss to coat thoroughly.

3. In a small bowl, use a fork to beat the egg white with salt until frothy. Pour over the oats and mix very well.

4. Spread granola on the baking sheet. Use your fingers to clump the granola. Bake for 20 minutes. Turn with a spatula, then bake for 20 to 25 minutes more, until the granola clusters are golden brown on the edges. Cool on the baking sheet without stirring.

5. Mix cooled granola clusters with pepitas, chocolate chunks, dried cherries, raisins and coconut, if using. Store in an airtight container at room temperature for up to 2 weeks.

Tahini Maple Tea Cookies

Afternoon tea is a lifelong habit of mine, and I am always looking for a healthy accompaniment that also packs a wallop of flavour. I first discovered how much I enjoy tahini and maple together during a smoothie kick—and decided to marry them in a cookie.

I call this a tea cookie because it is not overly sweet and it pairs well with a spiced chai. They are also a lunch box staple around here, nut-free and substantial enough to provide a little energy for my boys. I find that their flavour deepens and develops over a few days.

Pull up a stool and invite the kids to help with the stirring, rolling and pressing of the cookies—it's fun for the whole family.

4 tablespoons (60 mL) unsalted butter

⅓ cup (75 mL) tahini

½ cup (125 mL) dark muscovado sugar or dark brown sugar

¼ cup (60 mL) pure maple syrup

½ teaspoon (2 mL) pure vanilla extract

1 medium egg

1 cup (250 mL) whole wheat pastry flour

½ cup (125 mL) all-purpose flour

½ teaspoon (2 mL) baking soda

½ teaspoon (2 mL) sea salt

1 teaspoon (5 mL) ground cinnamon

½ teaspoon (2 mL) ground cardamom

Pinch of ground cloves

¼ cup (60 mL) toasted sesame seeds

1. Position oven racks in the upper and lower thirds of the oven and preheat oven to 350°F (180°C). Line two rimmed baking sheets with parchment paper.

2. In a small saucepan, melt butter with tahini and whisk until smooth. Scrape the mixture into a large bowl. Add the sugar, maple syrup, vanilla and egg. Cream the batter with a wooden spoon until thoroughly blended.

3. In another bowl, whisk together the whole wheat flour, all-purpose flour, baking soda, salt, cinnamon, cardamom and cloves. Tip into the butter mixture and fold together to combine into a soft dough.

4. Using your hands, roll the dough into 24 1½-inch (4 cm) balls and place them on the baking sheets about 2 inches (5 cm) apart. Use a fork to press them down once, then dip the edges in sesame seeds and return to the baking sheets.

5. Bake for 9 minutes, or until lightly golden on the bottoms, rotating the pans halfway through. Transfer the cookies to a wire rack and cool completely. Store in an airtight container at cool room temperature for up to 4 days.

Pepper Parmesan Crackers

MAKES 6 DOZEN · REQUIRES TIME FOR PREP

❧

Here's what is good to know about making crackers. First, the dough comes together in mere seconds with the help of a food processor. Second, you have to roll and cut out every single one. So I suggest you enlist little hands to help if you can!

My kids love making these crackers almost as much as they love eating them. One Christmas we made about six batches and gave them to the boys' schoolteachers along with a small wheel of Brie. Now that was a successful homemade gift idea.

1 cup (250 mL) whole wheat pastry flour

1 cup (250 mL) all-purpose flour

1 teaspoon (5 mL) sea salt

1 teaspoon (5 mL) finely ground black pepper

½ teaspoon (2 mL) dry mustard

½ teaspoon (2 mL) garlic powder

¾ cup (175 mL) cold unsalted butter, cubed

⅔ cup (150 mL) freshly grated Parmesan cheese

6 to 8 tablespoons (90 to 125 mL) ice water

1. In a food processor, combine the whole wheat flour, all-purpose flour, salt, pepper, and mustard and garlic powder. Pulse a couple of times to combine. Add the cold butter cubes and process for about 10 seconds, until the mixture resembles coarse crumbs. Add the Parmesan and blitz the processor once or twice to combine. Add the water, a few tablespoons at a time, and pulse the processor until tiny moist clumps form. You may not need all the water.

2. Turn dough out onto a clean counter and press into two flattened discs. Wrap well with plastic wrap and refrigerate for 30 minutes or overnight.

3. Preheat oven to 375°F (190°C).

4. On a lightly floured counter, roll the dough into a large circle about ⅛ inch (3 mm) thick. Cut out small circles with a cookie cutter or a shot glass and place on a rimmed baking sheet about 1 inch (2.5 cm) apart. Stab each cracker twice with a fork.

5. Bake for 11 to 13 minutes, until the crackers start to brown ever so slightly around the edges. Transfer crackers to a wire rack and cool completely. Store in an airtight container in a cool place for up to 2 weeks or freeze for up to 6 months.

Homegrown Vegetarian

❧

❧

It was always my plan to have our backyard garden be the hub of our little urban homestead, but it was a nice surprise when it worked out that way. From early spring to late fall, we all gravitate toward the raised beds in the evenings and linger for as long as we can.

Danny perches on the wide, worn edges and pulls weeds (now that he's learned to tell them apart from vegetable seedlings!). Clara is always hunting for a snack, whether a handful of pea pods, sweet cherry tomatoes or a freshly pulled baby carrot. The boys are never still; they brandish sticks and engage in an imaginary lightsaber battle on the garden's edge. Even the animals join in. Our cats sprawl out lazily and sun themselves next to the parsley.

The summer days are long and hot, filled with chores that never quite seem to finish. But occasionally in the late afternoon, when the sun has slanted down into the trees and the children's feet are starting to tire, Danny and I cool down with a Herbal Homestead Gin and Tonic (page 135) that I mix in the garden, using ingredients I harvest straight from the vine. Then I thin the lettuce beds for a bowl of Summer Greens with Grilled Avocado (page 106), pluck peppers for a Tofu Vegetable Stir-Fry with Cashews (page 121) and head to the kitchen to prep dinner while Danny joins in on the boys' Jedi fun.

We eat a diet rich in fresh vegetables, thanks to a backyard garden and local farm stands that keep me inspired from April through November. Over the winter months we thrive on winter squash, root vegetables and brassicas, as well as greens from a weekly basket of local greenhouse-grown produce from Lufa Farms (lufa.com). Tending the backyard garden is a big part of our family food culture. Each year, the children have hands-on experience growing and harvesting yard-to-table produce. As a result, they have a healthy respect for where produce comes from and the effort it takes to yield even a single basket. It's also been helpful in teaching them to eat with the seasons and the benefits that come with that practice. Even if you don't grow a few vegetables on the patio or balcony, you can still develop a healthy food culture for your family by providing a bounty of wholesome foods and teaching your children about seasonal and local eating.

No matter the time of year, vegetables infuse our family meals with textures, colours and flavours. In summer we stuff an abundance of sweet peppers with spinach lasagna (page 117) and whizz cucumbers with tomatoes into a refreshing Chilled Cucumber Tomato Soup (page 109). I pair tangy rhubarb with sweet plums for my children's absolute favourite sorbet (page 132), and peaches languish on the grill before I sandwich them in a shortcake (page 137). It's a luxurious season, no doubt about it.

In the colder months, we roast beets for Spaghetti with Beet Rosé Sauce (page 128) and fold smashed rutabaga into fluffy mashed potatoes for topping a hearty Lentil Cottage Pie with Rutabaga Mash (page 123). Root vegetables are slowly stewed in apple cider and bolstered with creamy chickpeas for a comforting Slow Cooker Root Vegetable Cider Stew (page 131). The dishes are heartier in winter, but every bit as flavourful.

As you can imagine, the children aren't quite as keen on vegetable-based mains as Danny and I are. Over the years (eleven and counting), I've learned to work the vegetables into our meals in creative ways that receive two thumbs up from everyone around the table.

Vegetarian dishes are front and centre at so many of our meals, they deserve a chapter of their own. For lunch, dinner or dessert, these recipes will show you how to let vegetables shine all year round and keep your family coming back for more.

Slow-Roasted Tomato and Ricotta Tartines

I make up for my dislike of sun-dried tomatoes with absolute love for the slow-roasted version. Every summer gathering in my backyard calls for a tray or two, served up on ricotta-topped toast. Over and over again, the sophisticated yet simple slow-roasted tomato wins new converts.

To make the most of the oven during the hot summer months, pack it with as many trays of tomatoes as will fit. Layer the extra slow-roasted tomatoes in jars with herbs, garlic and olive oil and freeze them for winter. They reconstitute beautifully for pizza, sandwiches and pasta.

4 large tomatoes, cored

4 tablespoons (60 mL) extra-virgin olive oil, divided

4 teaspoons (20 mL) balsamic vinegar, divided

½ teaspoon (2 mL) freshly ground black pepper, divided

1 baguette

1 batch Lighter Ricotta (page 224) or 1¼ cups (300 mL) store-bought

About 12 fresh basil leaves, minced

1 teaspoon (5 mL) fresh thyme leaves, minced

½ teaspoon (2 mL) fine sea salt

1. Preheat oven to 225°F (110°C) with a rack in the middle. Line a rimmed baking sheet with parchment paper.

2. Slice tomatoes lengthwise in ½-inch (1 cm) rounds and arrange them in a single layer on the baking sheet. Brush with about 1 tablespoon (15 mL) of the olive oil and 2 teaspoons (10 mL) of the balsamic vinegar, then sprinkle lightly with ¼ teaspoon (1 mL) pepper.

3. Slow-roast the tomatoes for 5 to 6 hours. Ovens vary, so start checking in on them after 2 to 3 hours. When they're done, they will have shrivelled slightly and partially dried, but still be soft to the touch. Remove from oven and brush lightly with the remaining 2 teaspoons (10 mL) balsamic vinegar. Cool tomatoes on the baking sheet until room temperature. Transfer to a platter.

4. Increase the oven temperature to 350°F (180°C). Cut the baguette into ½-inch (1 cm) slices and arrange on the same baking sheet. Brush tops generously with the remaining 3 tablespoons (45 mL) olive oil. Bake for 10 minutes, or until the bread is light golden. Remove from oven and cool completely.

5. Whip Lighter Ricotta with minced basil and thyme, sea salt and the remaining ¼ teaspoon (1 mL) pepper. Spread toasted baguette with a spoonful of herbed ricotta. Top with a slow-roasted tomato slice. Repeat until you have a platter of tartines. Serve.

Summer Greens with Grilled Avocado

SERVES 4

❧

I owe the now defunct *Gourmet* magazine all the credit for introducing me to the grilled avocado and its seductive smokiness. It now frequents many a salad over the summer months, such as this recipe that features the thinnings from my lettuce patch and the English peas that Clara picks and shells herself. This salad is best assembled when you are already grilling dinner, because the avocado needs only a few minutes on the heat. Oh, and while you're at it, try grilling the red onion, too. Delicious!

Don't stop making this salad when the spring greens and the pea plants whither in the summer heat; use romaine hearts instead and toss an ear of corn onto the grill along with the avocado.

Dressing

1 small clove garlic, crushed

1 tablespoon (15 mL) red wine vinegar

½ teaspoon (2 mL) Dijon mustard

½ teaspoon (2 mL) liquid honey

½ teaspoon (2 mL) sea salt

¼ teaspoon (1 mL) freshly ground black pepper

3 tablespoons (45 mL) extra-virgin olive oil, plus more for grilling

Salad

¼ small red onion

2 avocados

10 heaping cups (2.5 L) spring greens

1 cup (250 mL) fresh English peas

¼ cup (60 mL) sunflower seeds, toasted

1. **MAKE THE DRESSING** In a small bowl, whisk together the garlic, red wine vinegar, mustard, honey, salt and pepper. While whisking, drizzle in the olive oil, whisking until creamy.

2. **MAKE THE SALAD** Slice the red onion into slivers. Cut avocados in half; remove and discard pits. Place the avocados cut side down on the cutting board, cut each half in half again, and peel off and discard the skin. Brush lightly with olive oil on all sides.

3. Place avocado quarters on a very clean grill (they can stick if the rack is dirty) and grill for about 2 minutes per edge. Remove and cool.

4. Toss the greens with 3 tablespoons (45 mL) of the dressing. Tumble in the green peas, toasted sunflower seeds and sliced red onion. Toss again. Divide the salad among four bowls and arrange two grilled avocado quarters on top of each. Drizzle the remainder of the dressing on the avocado and serve the salads at once.

Chilled Cucumber Tomato Soup

SERVES 4 · REQUIRES TIME FOR PREP

Cold soup. I know, it's almost a contradiction. Isn't soup supposed to be a comforting dish, warming us down to our very toes? Well yes, but cold soup is a marvellously refreshing way to enjoy summer's produce as well as an easy way to get the kids to eat their vegetables.

This quick vegan soup requires just a bowl and a blender and packs a wallop of flavour. Keep it in the fridge for no-fuss light lunches all week long or serve it up as shooters for a summer gathering. Keep in mind that your soup is only as good as your produce, so choose vine-ripened vegetables in their prime.

6 medium yellow tomatoes, cored and quartered

1 English cucumber, peeled and roughly chopped

3 tablespoons (45 mL) rice vinegar

1 teaspoon (5 mL) agave syrup

½ teaspoon (2 mL) fine sea salt

Herbed Croutons (page 159), for garnish

Microgreens, for garnish

1. Toss the tomatoes and cucumber in a bowl with the rice vinegar and agave. Cover with a clean tea towel and macerate at room temperature for 1 to 3 hours.

2. Tip the vegetables into a blender, along with all the accumulated juices. Sprinkle in the salt. Purée until very smooth. Chill for at least an hour. Pour soup into chilled cups or bowls and serve with a garnish of Herbed Croutons and microgreens. The soup will keep in the refrigerator for up to 3 days. The liquid and the pulp will separate while it sits, so be sure to shake, whisk or blend well before serving.

TIP: *The soup makes a fine base for a variety of exciting garnishes. Try diced avocado or baby cucumber, or chopped chives or basil. Play around with baby radishes and cherry tomatoes with a crumbling of feta.*

Vietnamese Summer Rolls

SERVES 4

❧

Sometime between four and five years of age, my eldest, Noah, got hooked on Thai-style summer rolls, packed with greens, rice noodles and vegetables. His siblings soon followed his enthusiastic lead, so I taught them all how to roll their own.

In summer we snip our own mint and cilantro from the garden; if I'm growing Thai basil we gather some of that, too. We pull carrots, pick a cucumber and snip lettuce leaves. Then we wash, chop, shred and assemble these summer rolls together for a healthy family meal that celebrates yard-to-table eating. Feel free to customize the fillings to suit your tastes.

Peanut Sauce

½ cup (125 mL) natural peanut butter

1 small clove garlic, crushed

2 tablespoons (30 mL) hoisin sauce

1 tablespoon (15 mL) liquid honey

⅓ cup (75 mL) coconut water or filtered water

1 tablespoon (15 mL) tamari soy sauce

1 tablespoon (15 mL) freshly squeezed lime juice

Vietnamese summer rolls

4 ounces (115 g) brown rice vermicelli

1 tablespoon (15 mL) tamari soy sauce

1 teaspoon (5 mL) sesame oil

1 medium English cucumber

1 red bell pepper

1 bunch baby carrots, scrubbed

1 bunch baby romaine lettuce

12 to 14 rice paper wrappers (8½-inch/21 cm diameter)

1 bunch fresh cilantro

1 small bunch fresh mint

1. **MAKE THE PEANUT SAUCE** In a medium bowl, cream together the peanut butter, crushed garlic, hoisin and honey until it is a smooth paste. Pour in coconut water, tamari and lime juice and whisk until smooth. Keep at room temperature until ready to serve.

2. **MAKE THE VIETNAMESE SUMMER ROLLS** Bring a medium pot of water to a boil and drop in the rice noodles. Turn off heat and soak noodles until they are tender, about 5 minutes. Drain and cool completely. Toss noodles with the tamari and sesame oil.

3. Prepare the vegetables by cutting thin strips of cucumber, bell pepper and carrot and tearing the lettuce; keep these in separate piles.

4. Half fill a wide bowl with warm water for soaking the rice paper wrappers. Spread a damp tea towel on the counter. Add a rice paper wrapper to the warm water and soak for 1 to 2 minutes, until it is softened. Spread it out flat on the tea towel. Heap a few tablespoons of the seasoned rice vermicelli on the lower third of the rice paper. Build a little stack of assorted vegetables on the noodles. Tear off a few leaves of herbs and add them on top. Fold the bottom of the sticky rice

paper up and fold in the sides to cover the vegetable stack. Roll up toward the top of the rice paper, compressing as you go, until you have your summer roll. This takes practice, so be patient; you will improve with each roll. Place the roll on a platter and cover with another damp tea towel to keep moist.

5.   Keep assembling and rolling until all the fillings are used up. Serve at once with Peanut Sauce.

Harvest Corn Chowder

During sweet corn season it is perfectly acceptable to enjoy corn no other way than on the cob with salted butter and black pepper, but if you should ever tire of that delight, this soup needs to be first on the list to make. It's a lighter version of corn chowder, packed with the best vegetables of the summer season. You won't even miss the bacon—honest!—because this soup bursts with fresh flavour, thanks to a homemade corn stock that uses the leftover cobs.

The fresher the corn, the sweeter it is, so try to buy your cobs on the same day you intend to make this soup. Also, the chowder is vegetarian and gluten-free and can be adapted to be vegan if the cream is replaced with a little coconut or cashew milk; either would be delicious.

3 fresh corn cobs

2 sprigs fresh thyme, divided

1 bay leaf

1 clove garlic, peeled

3 cups (750 mL) water

1 Thai chili (optional)

1 tablespoon (15 mL) extra-virgin olive oil

1 small sweet onion, such as Vidalia, diced

2 small zucchini, green and yellow

1 small red bell pepper

1 cup (250 mL) diced red potatoes

½ cup (125 mL) heavy (35%) cream

1 teaspoon (5 mL) sea salt

¼ teaspoon (1 mL) freshly ground black pepper

1. **MAKE THE STOCK** Working with one ear of corn at a time, wedge the pointy end into the hole of a Bundt pan. Holding the top of the cob firmly, use a knife to slice from top to bottom, letting the blade run right along the cob. The kernels will fall into the Bundt pan for easy collecting. Reserve the kernels.

2. Combine the corn cobs, 1 sprig of thyme, bay leaf, garlic and water in a large pot. Add a fresh Thai chili if you want a spicy stock. Bring to a boil, then reduce heat to low and simmer, uncovered, for an hour. Strain stock and discard the solids. Use at once or store for up to 5 days in the refrigerator.

3. **MAKE THE CHOWDER** In a large pot, warm the olive oil over medium heat. Add the onion and cook for 5 minutes, stirring occasionally. Meanwhile, slice zucchini lengthwise into quarters, then thickly slice. Halve, seed and chop the red pepper. Add the zucchini, red pepper and remaining sprig of thyme to the onion. Cook for another 5 minutes, stirring occasionally.

4. Pour in about 2½ cups (625 mL) of the corn stock and add potatoes. Simmer chowder over medium-low heat for 15 minutes, or until the potatoes are tender. Add reserved corn kernels, cream, salt and pepper. Simmer until piping hot, about 5 more minutes. Remove the thyme sprig and serve.

Gardener's Sloppy Joes

SERVES 6

❧

After a morning of working in the garden, I often crave something more substantial than a salad for lunch, but I still want something nourishing. These lentil sloppy joes are a filling, frugal and totally satisfying meatless main. Even the kids like them, especially served up on a toasted bun with homemade Garlicky Sandwich Pickles (page 264). I love to scoop a little avocado onto mine and top it with garden greens.

Lentils are one of my favourite dry pantry staples to have around (see How to Cook Pulses, page 237), and this recipe demonstrates that they are not just for winter. The filling freezes very well, which means you can rely on a reheat and stay in the garden longer.

1 tablespoon (15 mL) extra-virgin olive oil

1 small onion, diced

1 red or yellow bell pepper, diced

2 stalks celery, finely chopped

1 teaspoon (5 mL) ground cumin

1 teaspoon (5 mL) chili powder

1 cup (250 mL) French green lentils, rinsed and drained

3 cups (750 mL) Basic Vegetable Stock (page 231) or water

1 can (28 ounces/796 mL) tomato sauce

3 tablespoons (45 mL) tomato paste

1 teaspoon (5 mL) hot sauce, or to taste

2 teaspoons (10 mL) balsamic vinegar

1 teaspoon (5 mL) sea salt

6 whole wheat or sprouted grain buns, sliced in half

Toppings: relish; pickles; avocado; coleslaw; sliced onions

1. Heat the olive oil in a medium, heavy pot over medium heat. Add diced onion, bell pepper and celery. Cook, stirring occasionally, until they soften, about 5 minutes. Sprinkle in cumin and chili powder; cook for an additional minute.

2. Add the lentils, Basic Vegetable Stock, tomato sauce, tomato paste and hot sauce. Increase heat to high and bring to a boil. Reduce heat to medium-low and cook, uncovered and stirring occasionally, for about 30 minutes. Add water if the liquid level falls below the lentils. Taste the lentils, and once they are sufficiently tender, stir in the balsamic vinegar and salt.

3. Lightly toast the buns and butter them if you wish. Serve buns and lentils together and let people scoop their own sloppy joes. Serve with an assortment of toppings. Store lentils in an airtight container in the refrigerator for up to 4 days or freeze for up to 6 months. These lentils reheat very well, making them an ideal meal to take to others.

Spinach Lasagna Stuffed Sweet Peppers

SERVES 4

This recipe was an experiment to incorporate more vegetables into our diet, and it was an instant hit. I mean, everyone loves lasagna, right? Not only are these individual vegetarian lasagnas a great do-ahead weeknight meal, but they're also one of my favourite recipes for summertime entertaining. They feel indulgent, but not heavy, because the sweet bell peppers are really the stars of the show. Serve with crusty bread and a salad.

2 teaspoons (10 mL) unsalted butter

3 ounces (85 g) baby spinach

¾ cup (175 mL) Lighter Ricotta (page 224) or store-bought

½ teaspoon (2 mL) fine sea salt

¼ teaspoon (1 mL) freshly ground black pepper

4 medium bell peppers, any colour, washed

1 cup (250 mL) tomato sauce

2 fresh lasagna sheets

1½ cups (375 mL) grated mozzarella cheese

Fresh basil, for garnish

1. Preheat oven to 400°F (200°C) if you plan on baking the stuffed peppers right away.

2. In a medium saucepan, melt the butter over medium heat. Add the spinach and cook only until it is wilted, about 2 minutes. Transfer the spinach to a fine-mesh sieve and press out the excess liquid. Chop the cooked spinach and transfer to a small bowl. Add the Lighter Ricotta, salt and pepper. Mix well and taste for sufficient seasoning.

3. Cut bell peppers in half lengthwise and scoop out the seeds. Lightly oil a 13- × 9-inch (3.5 L) baking pan and place the pepper halves in it, cut side up. Spoon 1 tablespoon (15 mL) of tomato sauce into each of the peppers. Top that with a small square of lasagna sheet. Divide the spinach mixture among the peppers. Sprinkle half of the mozzarella into all the peppers. Repeat with another layer of lasagna sheets and a topping of tomato sauce. Finish with the remaining mozzarella. At this point the stuffed peppers can be refrigerated for up to 8 hours.

4. Bake for 35 to 40 minutes or until the peppers are tender when pierced with a knife. Cool slightly before serving—these mini lasagnas will be very hot on the inside. Top with fresh basil if desired.

TIP: *Look for bell peppers with four lobes on the bottom, as these sit flatter in the pan once they have been halved.*

Roasted Tomato and Lentil Soup

SERVES 6

An abundance of paste tomatoes at the end of summer inspires many dishes in my kitchen, like this nourishing take on classic tomato soup. There are always garden carrots hanging around, too, and flourishing herbs, so into the pot they go.

I roast trays of tomatoes and simmer big batches of soup to freeze for winter or swap with friends (see "How to Host a Soup Swap," page 140). The soup keeps for 6 months in the freezer and reheats beautifully. On a chilly January day, there are few pleasures as enjoyable as this soup dotted with a spoonful of Basil and Pepita Pesto (page 247) or my Herbed Croutons (page 159).

12 ripe tomatoes, cored and halved lengthwise

4 cloves garlic, peeled

3 small carrots, peeled and roughly chopped

2 tablespoons (30 mL) extra-virgin olive oil

½ teaspoon (2 mL) freshly ground black pepper

1 tablespoon (15 mL) fresh thyme leaves

1 cup (250 mL) water

¾ cup (175 mL) red lentils, rinsed and drained

2 cups (500 mL) Basic Vegetable Stock (page 231)

2 teaspoons (10 mL) balsamic vinegar

1 teaspoon (5 mL) sea salt, or to taste

1. Preheat oven to 400°F (200°C). Place the tomato halves, garlic and carrots in a roasting pan or rimmed baking sheet lined with parchment. Drizzle with the olive oil. Sprinkle with pepper and thyme leaves. Roast vegetables for 45 minutes. A little caramelization on the tomatoes is fine.

2. Working in two batches, carefully transfer the vegetables to a food processor or blender and blend until smooth. Pour the mixture into a medium saucepan. Add the water to the blender and "rinse" the tomato sauce out. Add this tomato water to the pot as well.

3. Stir in the lentils and Basic Vegetable Stock. Bring to a boil over high heat. Reduce heat to low and simmer, partially covered and stirring occasionally, until the lentils are tender, 30 to 40 minutes.

4. Stir in the balsamic vinegar and salt. Taste the soup and add a dash of additional salt if desired. Serve soup with a dollop of yogurt or Basil and Pepita Pesto or topped with Herbed Croutons.

Tofu Vegetable Stir-Fry with Cashews

SERVES 4 TO 6

In all honesty, I tried quite a few different ways of cooking tofu before I hit upon one that my children enjoyed as much as I did. Firm tofu is key for pleasing kids, as are the bold flavours of lime, sesame and soy sauce. We enjoy this stir-fry over Basic Brown Rice Pilaf (page 235) and frequently change up the snow peas for broccoli.

Snow peas are also known as Chinese pea pods, since they are often used in stir-fries. The whole pod is edible, although the tough string along the edge should be pulled off before eating. And be sure to look for organic tofu, as other versions are made with GMO soy.

1 pound (450 g) firm organic tofu	½ teaspoon (2 mL) cornstarch	1 large clove garlic, minced
1 lime, halved	½ pound (225 g) snow peas	Pinch of sea salt
3 tablespoons (45 mL) tamari soy sauce, divided	1 small red bell pepper	2 teaspoons (10 mL) canola oil, divided
3 tablespoons (45 mL) sesame oil, divided	1 small yellow bell pepper	½ cup (125 mL) raw cashews
	1 tablespoon (15 mL) liquid honey	

1. Slice the tofu into strips about ½ inch (1 cm) thick and 1 inch (2.5 cm) wide. Lay tofu on a paper towel and pat dry. Press the tofu with another paper towel to remove excess moisture.

2. In a medium bowl, mix together a marinade of the juice of ½ lime, 1 tablespoon (15 mL) tamari, 1 tablespoon (15 mL) sesame oil and cornstarch. Add the tofu and toss gently to coat. Marinate for 15 minutes while you prepare the vegetables.

3. Trim the stem from the snow peas and pull off the string that runs down the side of the pod. Cut bell peppers in half and discard the seeds. Slice peppers into ½-inch (1 cm) strips.

4. Whisk together a sauce of the juice of the remaining ½ lime, remaining 2 tablespoons (30 mL) tamari, 1 tablespoon (15 mL) sesame oil and honey. Stir in minced garlic and set aside.

(recipe continues)

5. Drain the tofu from the marinade and pat dry again; season lightly with salt. Heat 1 teaspoon (5 mL) of the canola oil in a large, well-seasoned wok or nonstick skillet over medium-high heat. When oil is very hot, add half of the tofu and cook for 2 to 3 minutes on one side, until lightly golden. Turn the pieces of tofu and brown them on the other side. Transfer to a plate. Heat the remaining 1 teaspoon (5 mL) canola oil and repeat with the remaining tofu.

6. Increase heat to high, add the remaining 1 tablespoon (15 mL) sesame oil to the wok and tumble in the prepared vegetables. Stir-fry for 4 to 5 minutes, until the colours are bright and the bell peppers start to soften.

7. Return the browned tofu to the pan and pour over the reserved tamari sauce mixture. Tumble in the cashews. Stir-fry, stirring constantly, until the sauce has thickened and coated everything, about 2 to 3 minutes. Remove from heat and serve at once.

Lentil Cottage Pie with Rutabaga Mash

SERVES 6

A hearty lentil pie is a regular dish on our dinner table, and I frequently change up the mash topping. Cauliflower purée is delicious in season, and mashed sweet potatoes, too. But in winter, when we are craving comfort food, I make a combination of potatoes and rutabaga that makes everyone happy. Rutabaga is mild, yet it has an earthiness that complements the sweet corn and the meaty lentils. For an extra-creamy mash, cook the rutabaga in milk and finish with a little cream cheese.

Be sure to serve this cottage pie with a jar of something puckery from the pantry. I heap Simple Sauerkraut (page 268) next to mine, and the children go with ketchup all the way.

1 tablespoon (15 mL) extra-virgin olive oil

1 medium onion, finely chopped

1 stalk celery, finely chopped

1 cup (250 mL) French green lentils, rinsed and drained

2¼ cups (550 mL) water

½ teaspoon (2 mL) dried thyme

1 medium rutabaga (about 1½ pounds/675 g)

2 teaspoons (10 mL) fine sea salt, divided

1½ pounds (675 g) potatoes

2 tablespoons (30 mL) unsalted butter

¼ cup (60 mL) whole milk or table (18%) cream

2 tablespoons (30 mL) Slow Cooker Tomato Ketchup (page 279) or store-bought

1 teaspoon (5 mL) Worcestershire sauce

½ teaspoon (2 mL) ground cumin

½ teaspoon (2 mL) tamari soy sauce

5 drops hot sauce

Freshly ground black pepper

1 cup (250 mL) fresh or frozen sweet corn kernels

1. Heat the olive oil in a medium saucepan over medium-high heat. Add onion and celery and sauté for 5 minutes, or until they are soft and slightly translucent. Add the lentils and water. Sprinkle in the thyme. Bring to a simmer, then reduce heat to medium and cook, uncovered, for 20 to 25 minutes, until lentils are tender. Remove from heat.

2. While the lentils are cooking, trim off the top and bottom of the rutabaga. Stand it upright and cut away the peel using a chef's knife. Cut the flesh into ½-inch (1 cm) pieces (any larger and it will take forever to cook). Place rutabaga in a pot and cover with cold water. Add 1 teaspoon (5 mL) of the salt and bring to a boil. Reduce heat and simmer for about 30 minutes.

(recipe continues)

3. Meanwhile, peel the potatoes and cut into ½-inch (1 cm) chunks. When the rutabaga is fork-tender but still a bit firm, add the potatoes. Cook until both vegetables are tender enough to be mashed with the back of a fork, about another 15 minutes. Drain and mash thoroughly. (A food processor is helpful for speeding this up.) Stir in the butter, milk and ½ teaspoon (2 mL) of the salt.

4. Return to the lentils and add the Slow Cooker Tomato Ketchup, Worcestershire sauce, cumin, tamari, hot sauce, the remaining ½ teaspoon (2 mL) salt and black pepper to taste. Stir to combine. Bring lentils to a simmer. Cook for another 5 minutes or so, stirring often, to let the flavours come together.

5. Preheat oven to 375°F (190°C).

6. Scrape seasoned lentils into a medium baking dish, spreading to cover the bottom. Top evenly with corn. Scoop the mashed vegetables on top and spread them evenly. Bake the cottage pie for about 30 minutes, until heated through. Serve hot.

Roasted Cauliflower with Quick Tomato Sauce

SERVES 4

In my kitchen, I often manage a surplus of tomatoes by simmering a batch of fresh tomato sauce as a base for our dinner. In this recipe I do a version of Marcella Hazan's famous tomato sauce (which works with both fresh and canned tomatoes) and use it to top another seasonal favourite: roasted cauliflower. Homemade Lighter Ricotta (page 224) and a sprinkling of fresh herbs complete the dish.

If your children are less enthusiastic about cauliflower, reserve a portion of the sauce and ricotta to toss with pasta and enjoy more cauliflower for yourself.

3 pounds (1.35 kg) fresh Roma tomatoes

⅓ cup (75 mL) unsalted butter

1 medium onion, peeled

1 teaspoon (5 mL) fine sea salt, divided

1 medium head of cauliflower

2 tablespoons (30 mL) extra-virgin olive oil

¼ cup (60 mL) Lighter Ricotta (page 224) or store-bought

Fresh basil or mint, for garnish

1. Preheat oven to 400°F (200°C).

2. Core the tomatoes and roughly chop into large pieces.

3. Melt the butter in a large saucepan over medium heat. When the butter is bubbling, tumble in the tomatoes and their juices. Cut onion into 4 wedges and add it to the pan along with ½ teaspoon (2 mL) of the salt. Cook down into a sauce, stirring occasionally, about 40 minutes.

4. Meanwhile, cut the cauliflower into medium-size florets. On a rimmed baking sheet, toss together cauliflower and olive oil until well coated. Season with remaining ½ teaspoon (2 mL) salt and toss again. Spread cauliflower in a single layer on the baking sheet and roast for 20 to 25 minutes, until the edges are browned and caramelized. You should be able to easily pierce the cauliflower with a fork.

5. Heap roasted cauliflower in a serving dish. Spoon the tomato sauce over the cauliflower. Top with Lighter Ricotta and finish with torn fresh basil.

Spaghetti with Beet Rosé Sauce

SERVES 4

≫

Roasted beets are a staple in my kitchen during the winter months. I regularly transform them into purée in my food processor to have on hand for favourite recipes such as this pasta sauce, a braised beet lentil dish and the chocolate cake from my first book. Puréed beets freeze very well, with almost no change in texture, so definitely roast and purée a big batch to stash for later. You can also find precooked beets in the deli section of many grocery stores.

This pasta is one of our weeknight staples, but topped with homemade Lighter Ricotta (page 224) and a few chopped walnuts, it's definitely worthy of a dinner party.

3 tablespoons (45 mL) salted butter

1 small onion, diced

1 bay leaf

1 cup (250 mL) beet purée (about 3 cooked medium red beets)

½ cup (125 mL) tomato sauce

½ cup (125 mL) heavy (35%) cream

½ teaspoon (2 mL) fine sea salt

¾ pound (340 g) whole wheat spaghetti

1 tablespoon (15 mL) chopped fresh flat-leaf parsley, for garnish

Freshly grated Parmesan cheese, for garnish

1. Melt the butter in a medium saucepan over medium-low heat. When it is bubbling, tumble in the onion and stir to coat. Add bay leaf and cook for a minute or so, until the onions soften slightly. Add the beet purée, tomato sauce and cream. Stir well. Reduce heat to low and simmer the sauce, uncovered and stirring occasionally, for 40 minutes. It should bubble slightly around the edges.

2. Meanwhile, bring a large pot of salted water to a boil. When the sauce is nearly finished, tip the spaghetti into the boiling water and cook according to package directions until al dente.

3. Reserve ½ cup (125 mL) of the pasta water, then drain the spaghetti and return it to the pot. Pour the beet sauce and the reserved pasta water over the spaghetti and stir well to coat. Serve immediately garnished with chopped parsley and freshly grated Parmesan.

Slow Cooker Root Vegetable Cider Stew

A resolution to cook more from my pantry inspired this autumn stew. It combines many ingredients I keep on hand, such as canned chickpeas, tomato sauce, onions and spices, along with root vegetables, into a comforting vegetarian stew. Cubes of turnip and parsnip simmer slowly in a sauce spiced with garam masala and turn into buttery bites that hold their shape nicely. Golden raisins plump up to become almost as big as the creamy chickpeas. Nearly a pint of fresh-pressed apple cider adds both acidity and sweetness to the dish, and a sprinkling of pistachios completes the stew.

Serve it up as is or with a wedge of crusty bread, and add a dollop of yogurt for good measure. It's even better on the second day, after the flavours have had an opportunity to mingle.

2 medium turnips (about ½ pound/225 g)

2 large parsnips

2 teaspoons (10 mL) Golden Ghee (page 223) or unsalted butter, divided

1 medium sweet onion, diced

2 cloves garlic, minced

1 teaspoon (5 mL) garam masala

1 teaspoon (5 mL) sea salt, divided

1 can (19 ounces/540 mL) chickpeas, rinsed and drained

1½ cups (375 mL) fresh-pressed apple cider (unfiltered raw apple juice)

1 cup (250 mL) tomato sauce

½ cup (125 mL) golden raisins

Chopped pistachios, for garnish

Full-fat plain organic yogurt, for topping (optional)

1. Peel the turnip and cut into ½-inch (1 cm) cubes. Peel the parsnips and cut them slightly larger. In a medium saucepan, melt 1 teaspoon (5 mL) of the Golden Ghee over medium heat. Slide in the onion, then stir and cook for 5 minutes, until softened. Sprinkle in the garlic and garam masala and cook for an additional minute.

2. Push the onions to the side of the pan and melt the remaining 1 teaspoon (5 mL) Golden Ghee. Tumble in the turnips and parsnips and stir to coat with the ghee. Toss in a pinch of salt and cook, stirring frequently, for 5 minutes.

3. Transfer the vegetables to a slow cooker. Add the chickpeas, cider, tomato sauce, raisins and remaining salt. Stir well. Cover with the lid and cook on low for 5 hours. Slow cookers vary, so check the stew after about 4 hours. The stew is ready when the turnip is tender but not mushy. Serve with a sprinkling of chopped pistachios and a spoonful of yogurt if you wish.

Rhubarb Plum Sorbet

SERVES 8 · REQUIRES TIME FOR PREP

❈

Juicy plums show up at the farm stands while my rhubarb patch is still flourishing, and so I pair them in the kitchen for a summertime dessert that is a pleasant balance of tart and sweet. I have a love for vanilla beans, but you could substitute a teaspoon of extract and still have a sensational dessert.

This sorbet comes together with minimal effort but does require a lengthy chill time, followed by a deep freeze. Thanks to the vodka, the sorbet stays soft and scoopable in the freezer. You can leave out the vodka, but the sorbet will freeze rock-hard. In that case, just remove it from the freezer 10 minutes before serving.

1½ cups (375 mL) raw cane sugar

2 cups (500 mL) water

5 medium red plums, pitted and sliced

1 cup (250 mL) diced rhubarb

1 vanilla bean, split lengthwise

3 tablespoons (45 mL) freshly squeezed lemon juice

1 teaspoon (5 mL) vodka

1. Combine sugar and water in a large saucepan. Bring to a boil over medium-high heat and stir until the sugar dissolves.

2. Gently tumble the plums and rhubarb into the sugar syrup. Scrape the seeds from the vanilla bean and add them, along with the vanilla pod. Reduce heat to medium and simmer the fruit for 10 to 12 minutes, so it cooks down and softens. Remove from heat. Remove the vanilla pod from the saucy fruit.

3. Carefully transfer the hot fruit and all the liquid to a blender. Cover the lid with a tea towel and blend until smooth. Transfer fruit purée to a bowl and cool completely. Cover the purée and chill overnight.

4. When ready to churn, pour lemon juice and vodka into the fruit purée and whisk well to incorporate. Follow your ice cream machine's instructions to churn purée into a soft sorbet. Transfer to a freezer-safe container and freeze for at least 4 hours before scooping and serving.

Herbal Homestead Gin and Tonic

Occasionally, on sultry summer afternoons, Danny and I cool down at cocktail hour with a drink that I mix right in the garden. This gin and tonic is our summertime drink of choice, thanks to its fragrant herbaceousness and cucumber sweetness. It is packed with an array of fresh herbs, all picked from my raised beds. I find it is best with a mix of mild herbs (parsley, basil, cilantro) and strong ones (thyme, oregano, tarragon), but feel free to customize your G&T to suit your taste.

It may sound strange, but a ripe, full-of-flavour tomato is essential, as it provides the necessary acidity to the drink. And you'll definitely want a cucumber that is more sweet than bitter, so taste it as you slice it. Muddling releases the juices in the vegetables and the fragrant oils in the herbs, before everything is topped up with gin, tonic and loads of ice for a cocktail that is as pretty as it is refreshing.

1 large vine-ripened tomato

3 inches (8 cm) of an English cucumber, unpeeled

½ cup (125 mL) loosely packed fresh herb leaves

2 cups (500 mL) ice cubes

2 to 4 ounces (60 to 125 mL) dry gin

1 bottle or can (9 ounces/275 mL) tonic water, well chilled

4 sprigs fresh herbs, for garnish

1. Core and roughly chop the tomato. Chop the cucumber into ½-inch (1 cm) chunks.

2. Divide the herb leaves between two sturdy 16-ounce highball glasses or pint (500 mL) mason jars. Tip equal parts chopped tomato and cucumber on top of the herbs. With a cocktail muddler, mash the herbs and vegetables into a perfumed pulp. It's okay if there are still a few larger pieces.

3. Fill the glasses three-quarters with ice and stir well with a long-handled bar spoon. Add 1 or 2 ounces (30 to 60 mL) of gin to each glass, depending on how boozy you like things. Top up glasses with tonic water and stir once. Garnish with a few fresh herb sprigs and enjoy immediately.

Grilled Peach Shortcakes with Rosemary-Honey Whipped Cream

SERVES 6 · REQUIRES TIME FOR PREP

When Ontario peaches are in season, we always have a basket or two ripening on the counter for snacking, making Noah's Peach Lemonade (page 169) and adding to salads. And when we can't wait for them to soften, I lay them on the grill after dinner, when the coals are dying down. Firm fruit is best for grilling, and letting them languish over slow heat intensifies the sweetness of the peaches, making them an ideal pairing for shortcake and cream.

There's no question that honey and peaches were meant for each other. Here I've sweetened both the whole wheat shortcake and the whipped cream with Rosemary-infused Honey, and finished the dessert with a little more drizzled on top. I've got pots of rosemary growing all over my patio, but you could infuse the honey with thyme or lavender, or just leave it as it is.

Rosemary-infused honey

⅔ cup (150 mL) liquid honey

2 sprigs fresh rosemary (about 5 inches/12 cm long)

Grilled peach shortcakes

1½ cups (375 mL) whole wheat pastry flour

1 teaspoon (5 mL) baking powder

½ teaspoon (2 mL) baking soda

½ teaspoon (2 mL) sea salt

6 tablespoons (90 mL) cold unsalted butter

½ cup (125 mL) Homemade Buttermilk (page 228) or store-bought

1 medium egg yolk

6 ripe freestone peaches, halved and pitted

1 cup (250 mL) heavy (35%) cream

1. **MAKE THE ROSEMARY-INFUSED HONEY** Heat honey in a small saucepan and add rosemary. Bring to a boil, then turn off heat and let infuse until cool. Remove rosemary and store honey in a small jar. This can be prepared up to a week in advance.

2. **MAKE THE SHORTCAKES** Preheat oven to 400°F (200°C) and line a rimmed baking sheet with parchment paper.

3. Into a large bowl, sift together the flour, baking powder, baking soda and salt. Using the large holes of a box grater, grate in the cold butter. Mix quickly with a fork or your fingers until the butter is evenly distributed.

4. In a measuring cup, beat the Homemade Buttermilk, egg yolk and 3 tablespoons (45 mL) of the Rosemary-infused Honey with a fork. Gradually add the buttermilk mixture to the dry ingredients, mixing gently to combine.

(recipe continues)

5. Turn dough out onto a lightly floured counter. With floured hands, pat dough into a circle 1 inch (2.5 cm) thick. Using a 2½-inch (6 cm) biscuit cutter, cut out 6 rounds. Transfer shortcakes to the prepared baking sheet.

6. Bake for 10 to 12 minutes, until lightly browned all over. Set aside to cool until ready to assemble the dessert.

7. GRILL THE PEACHES Preheat grill to 400°F (200°C). Place the peaches cut side down on the grill and cook for a few minutes until marked. Turn once, so the cut side is up, and transfer to an area with indirect heat. Reduce grill temperature to 300°F (150°C) and slowly grill the peaches for at least 1 hour. Peaches will be squishy soft and the pit cavern will be full of juice. In the last 10 minutes or so of cooking, brush peaches with 3 tablespoons of the Rosemary-infused Honey. Remove from grill and cool slightly.

8. ASSEMBLE THE GRILLED PEACH SHORTCAKES In a chilled bowl, whip the cream until soft peaks begin to form. Add 2 to 3 tablespoons (30 to 45 mL) of Rosemary-infused Honey, then continue whipping until the cream is firm yet still falls softly from the whisk.

9. Cut each shortcake in half horizontally. Place each bottom half on a plate or in a shallow bowl. Scoop a spoonful of whipped cream onto the base. Top with 2 grilled peach halves and another dollop of cream. Add the top half of the shortcake. Drizzle each dessert with ½ teaspoon (2 mL) or so Rosemary-infused Honey. Serve at once.

TIP: *Shortcakes can be frozen raw and baked up fresh when needed. They bake from frozen and will need about 16 minutes in the oven.*

HOW TO HOST A SOUP SWAP

I'm no stranger to food swaps. I've held a holiday cookie swap ever since I had a home to host it in, and my book *Brown Eggs and Jam Jars* has a section dedicated to the autumn preserve swap. Both are important events in my calendar, but the soup swap is steadily gaining my respect. It's so practical, and I love seeing the creations that my friends come up with. It also helps that I adore soup.

To me, the best time to host a soup swap is in the fall, when produce is in abundance, but a swap can also be a good excuse to bring people together during the cold winter months, when on some days soup feels like a necessity for survival.

As the host, plan to make a big pot of soup to enjoy during the event in addition to the soup you are swapping. I'm sure no one would complain if there were soft Whole Wheat Pita Breads (page 68) or Honey Whole Wheat Bagels (page 39) to accompany your soup, but only if baking is enjoyable for you. The whole goal of the soup swap is to make less work for you! Crackers and cheese would be just fine, too.

Six to seven guests are ideal, making for seven to eight varieties of soup including yours. Invite them in the absolute easiest way (group text, email, Facebook) and outline my suggestions as follows:

1. I recommend people bring 6 quarts (6 L) of soup to swap. It sounds like a lot of soup, but making a triple batch of soup really isn't that much more work than making one. The exception, of course, is if there's lots and lots of chopping. A lentil soup is the way to go, as are puréed soups.

2. Soups should be freezer-friendly. The good news is, nearly all soups freeze well. The ones that don't reheat well tend to be the soups with lots of dairy or potatoes.

3. Guests should arrive with the soup pre-measured into 1-quart (1 L) containers that they intend to give away. A wide-mouth mason jar or a clear plastic container is great. No toppings, please. If a recipe calls for a soup to be finished with croutons, cream, chopped fresh herbs or other topping, don't add it to the soup you are swapping.

4. If the soups are wildly creative, you may want to warm a bowl of each variety and let your guests sample a spoonful. I don't always bother with tasting if we have a lineup of classic soups like chicken noodle, beef and barley or carrot and ginger.

5. I like to have each guest pick a number. Number 1 selects their soup first, then I have the highest number choose their soup. Repeat until all the soup is gone.

6. Exchange the recipes, too. Have guests bring a handful of printouts of their recipe for guests to take home. This is also helpful if someone has an allergy or dietary concern and would like to scan the ingredients list. You may also discover a new favourite soup and wish to make it yourself. Now you'll have the recipe in hand.

Here are three soup suggestions to get you inspired to host your own soup swap: Josh's Borscht (page 88), Roasted Tomato and Lentil Soup (page 118) and Harvest Corn Chowder (page 113).

Fresh-Air Gatherings

Meals in summertime take place almost exclusively on our back patio. I travel back and forth between the grill and our long cedar table, while friends and family—a whole lot of family—gather to share another meal. Canadian summers are short, which is why we dine al fresco as much as possible during that coveted season. There's nothing like a warm summer evening to inspire one to host a gathering. It entreats us to fill the yard with friends, let the noise spill onto the neighbouring yards and throw the children's bedtime out the window. There's more finger food and fewer plates when we bring dinner out of doors; meals are less formal than in our dining room, but no less intimate.

For these meals, our food is fresh and vibrant, inspired by the region and the season. We stretch out dinner with platters of irresistible appetizers—warm grilled pitas (page 148) with tangy tzatziki (page 147) and baby cucumbers, or lemony pickled shrimp (page 152) and home-cured gravlax (page 151) on home-made crackers (page 98). This keeps everyone happy while the cumin-rubbed pork (page 165) or tequila-lime chicken (page 160) finishes up on the grill. Later we heap the grilled goods on large platters and serve them alongside Herbed Potato Salad with Preserved Lemons, Olives and Radishes (page 155) or Haidi's Caesar Salad (page 156). Happiness abounds.

My son Noah squeezes lemons and chopped peaches for his peach lemonade "invention" (page 169), then serves it up to all the thirsty children. For the adults, I keep a jar of Bloody Caesar mix (page 166) in the refrigerator, ready to shake up with ice and tequila and garnish with garden vegetables. For really spontaneous get-togethers, I scarcely do more than a pitcher of ice water infused with a handful of berries and a few sprigs of garden herbs.

During the week, dessert is seldom more complicated than local berries with soft whipped cream or a selection of Quebec melons with a squeeze of lime juice. But in August, when all the berries and stone fruits are in their prime, we host a pie social on a lazy Sunday afternoon and invite all our friends for a slice or three (page 179). Diets are broken and detoxes all but forgotten on this day; I have personally seen the toughest health regiment collapse when my Strawberry Rhubarb Pie (page 171) is on the picnic table. And with good reason! Good nutrition has a sweet side, too, as long as there is moderation and mindfulness.

Our family of five eats a lot of grilled chicken and Caesar salad in the summertime, rounded out with corn on the cob or a plate of fresh-picked carrots. This popular weeknight supper sounds fancier than it really is—it's fast and simple family food. It's also a meal that's easy to double or triple when friends stay through dinner.

This is my collection of vibrant summer recipes to share. Let it be a springboard for your own gatherings, large and small.

Classic Greek Tzatziki

MAKES 1½ CUPS (375 ML)

A while ago, my Greek friend, Christina, popped my bubble by explaining that classic Greek tzatziki didn't contain fresh dill, and she used white vinegar instead of lemon juice. Here's her recipe, as close as you will find to what's served at a Greek taverna. It's thick and creamy, with just the right amount of tang.

I like to serve tzatziki with cucumber spears and Oregano and Garlic Grilled Pitas (page 148). Add a bowl of olives and you have appetizers at the ready for your fresh-air feast.

½ English cucumber

1 small clove garlic, minced

1 cup (250 mL) labneh or plain Greek yogurt

2 tablespoons (30 mL) extra-virgin olive oil

1½ teaspoons (7 mL) white vinegar

½ teaspoon (2 mL) sea salt, or to taste

¼ teaspoon (1 mL) freshly ground black pepper, or to taste

1. Slice cucumber in half lengthwise and remove the seeds with a teaspoon. Each half will look like a canoe when you are finished. Grate the cucumber on the large holes of a box grater. Squeeze out the excess water with your hands.

2. In a bowl, combine grated cucumber, garlic, yogurt, olive oil, vinegar, salt and pepper. Mix well. Adjust seasoning if necessary. Cover and chill well.

3. Serve the tzatziki ice cold. Tzatziki will keep in an airtight container in the refrigerator for up to 3 days.

Oregano and Garlic Grilled Pitas

SERVES 4 TO 6

What could be better than grilled pita bread, bathed in a pungent garlic-infused olive oil, paired with a side of tangy Classic Greek Tzatziki (page 147) and a platter of cucumber spears? The combination of warm bread and cool tzatziki makes a lovely appetizer for summer gatherings.

2 cloves garlic

½ teaspoon (2 mL) sea salt

¼ cup (60 mL) extra-virgin olive oil

3 tablespoons (45 mL) fresh oregano leaves

8 Whole Wheat Pita Breads (page 68)

1.   Finely mince the garlic. Sprinkle with salt, and using the side of your knife, mash on the cutting board until you have a smooth paste.

2.   Heat olive oil in a small skillet over medium heat. Add the garlic paste and stir gently to distribute the paste throughout the oil. Turn off heat and let the oil cool to warm.

3.   Finely chop the oregano and stir it into the warm oil. Transfer infused herb oil to a small jar and reserve until ready to use. This can be done an hour or two in advance.

4.   Preheat grill to 400°F (200°C).

5.   Grill pitas over direct heat until grill marks appear. Turn once and grill on the other side. Remove from grill and brush both sides generously with garlic-oregano oil. Tuck pitas into a large square of foil to keep warm while you grill the remaining pitas.

6.   To serve, cut pitas into wedges. Serve warm with a side of tzatziki if desired.

Gin-Cured Gravlax

A summer long ago spent as a cook at a remote fishing resort equipped me with many ways to prepare fresh-caught salmon. As fast as the guides hauled the silver-skinned kings out of the Pacific, my fellow chef and I smoked, cured and cooked up the rich, luscious fish.

Once prepared, you can thinly slice the fish and serve it on crostini or Pepper Parmesan Crackers (page 98) with dollop of Lighter Ricotta (page 224). It's also delicious layered with thin slices of citrus segments and avocado on fresh Honey Whole Wheat Bagels (page 39).

1 small skin-on wild salmon fillet (about 1½ pounds/675 g)

⅓ cup (75 mL) gin

2 tablespoons (30 mL) black peppercorns

1 tablespoon (15 mL) coriander seeds

¾ cup (175 mL) coarse rock salt

½ cup (125 mL) raw cane sugar

6 or 7 sprigs fresh herbs such as rosemary or thyme, rinsed and patted dry

1. Place the salmon skin side down on a large plate and splash it with the gin, rubbing the alcohol all over the flesh. Let the gin soak into the fish for about 10 minutes.

2. Using a mortar and pestle, slightly crush the peppercorns and coriander seeds, leaving large chunks of both spices—you don't want a powder. In a large bowl, combine the salt, sugar and crushed spices. Snip the herb sprigs into smaller sections. To release their natural oils, bruise them slightly by rubbing the branches between your palms, and then add them to the salt mixture. Stir everything to combine.

3. Place the salmon skin side down on a wire rack set on a tray or rimmed baking sheet. Crust the top of the salmon generously with the spiced salt and heap with the herbs. Cover the surface of the fish tightly with plastic wrap. Place a baking sheet on top of the salmon and balance four or five cans on top to weigh it down. Refrigerate for at least 12 hours and up to 24 hours.

4. Scrape off and discard the salt crust and rinse the salmon well under cold running water. Pat the fish dry with a clean tea towel. Thinly slice the gravlax and serve as desired. Wrap any remaining gravlax tightly in plastic wrap and store in the refrigerator for up to 1 week.

TIP: *You don't have to limit this recipe to salmon; the curing method works well with Arctic char or trout. You can also use vodka in place of the gin.*

Pickled Shrimp with Bay Leaf and Lemon

SERVES 8 TO 10 · REQUIRES TIME FOR PREP

I've long been on a mission to eradicate the tasteless frozen shrimp cocktail ring from parties. This jar of pickled shrimp could do it single-handedly! The sherry vinegar adds a bit of sweetness to the brine, while the lemon juice brings a bright acidity to a memorable bite of seafood.

The shrimp are best pickled 2 or 3 days in advance. Then all you have to do when entertaining is pop open the lid, insert a fork or tongs and set out a stack of napkins. I like to serve them with a side of celery sticks or baby carrots. And try skewering a pickled shrimp and serve it atop a Bloody Caesar (page 166) for an unforgettable garnish.

¼ cup (60 mL) sherry vinegar

2 teaspoons (10 mL) kosher salt

2 teaspoons (10 mL) yellow mustard seeds

½ teaspoon (2 mL) celery seeds

2 shallots, thinly sliced

½ cup (125 mL) freshly squeezed lemon juice

¾ cup (175 mL) extra-virgin olive oil

1 pound (450 g) cooked, peeled and deveined cold-water shrimp (31–40 count)

½ lemon, cut into thin wedges

10 fresh bay leaves (or 2 or 3 dried)

1. In a small pot over medium heat, warm the sherry vinegar, salt, mustard seeds and celery seeds, stirring until the salt is dissolved. Remove from heat and stir in the sliced shallots. Cool completely. Stir in the lemon juice and olive oil.

2. In a clean 1-quart (1 L) wide-mouth jar, alternate layering 3 or 4 shrimp, 2 or 3 lemon wedges and a bay leaf. Pour the brine over the shrimp, making sure they are covered. Press the shrimp down gently with the back of a fork until submerged, if necessary.

3. Cover the jar with a clean lid and place in the refrigerator. Pickle the shrimp for at least a day and up to 3 days, turning the jar on its head once every 12 hours to evenly marinate the shrimp.

4. If you are serving the whole jar, bring it to room temperature first. If not, scoop out a few pickled shrimp and serve on toothpicks in a bowl.

Herbed Potato Salad with Preserved Lemons, Olives and Radishes

I've tried in vain to lure my children to the potato salad side of the picnic table, but they remain firmly planted next to their grandmother's classic pasta salad. That's fine—it means I can make a decidedly grown-up version complete with buttery olives, tangy preserved lemon and loads of fresh herbs. This is a French take on potato salad, which leaves out the mayo and embraces shallots, white wine vinegar, grainy mustard and a touch of tarragon.

2 pounds (900 g) red new potatoes

1 teaspoon (5 mL) sea salt, divided

2 tablespoons (30 mL) white wine vinegar

2 shallots, peeled

Juice of ½ lemon

¼ cup (60 mL) extra-virgin olive oil

2 teaspoons (10 mL) grainy mustard

¼ teaspoon (1 mL) freshly ground black pepper

1 bunch baby radishes

⅓ cup (75 mL) green olives, pitted

2 Preserved Meyer Lemons with Bay Leaf (page 263) or store-bought preserved lemons

2 tablespoons (30 mL) chopped fresh dill

2 tablespoons (30 mL) chopped fresh flat-leaf parsley

1 tablespoon (15 mL) chopped fresh tarragon

1. Slice the potatoes into ½-inch (1 cm) rounds and place in a large pot. Cover with cold water and add ½ teaspoon (2 mL) of the salt. Bring to a boil over high heat, then reduce heat and simmer until potatoes are al dente, 10 to 12 minutes. You want them to hold their shape but not have any crunch to them. Drain potatoes and spread on a tray or baking sheet to cool completely.

2. In a small saucepan, warm the white wine vinegar over medium heat for 1 or 2 minutes. Slice shallots into rings and stir them into the vinegar. Turn off heat; shallots will pickle slightly as the vinegar cools to room temperature. Add the lemon juice, olive oil, mustard, pepper and remaining ½ teaspoon (2 mL) salt. Whisk the vinaigrette until thoroughly combined.

3. Transfer the cooled potatoes to a large bowl. Slice the radishes and olives and toss them in. Remove and discard the flesh from the preserved lemons and thinly slice the peel. Add the lemon peel to the bowl.

4. Pour the vinaigrette over the potatoes and toss gently to coat. Sprinkle all the chopped dill, parsley and tarragon on top and give the salad one final stir. Heap onto a serving platter and serve at room temperature.

TIP: *The salad may be prepared in advance and refrigerated, but bring it back to room temperature before serving.*

Haidi's Caesar Salad

SERVES 8

In her twenties, my sister Haidi worked the floor of a fine-dining restaurant and made a version of this salad tableside every night. Occasionally we'd get lucky and she'd make it for us in all its tangy glory. My recipe is inspired by that remarkably zesty Caesar and is one salad that we never tire of eating. It is my children's most requested salad, making an appearance at birthdays, holidays and most every summer weekend gathering.

Use only fresh firm garlic, fresh lemon juice and the best Parmesan you can afford. Have your Herbed Croutons (page 159) made and the lettuce washed, dried and torn ahead of time, but prepare the rest of the salad just before serving. I toss my Caesar in an enormous wooden salad bowl, which, fittingly, was a wedding gift from Haidi.

2 cloves garlic, peeled

½ teaspoon (2 mL) kosher salt

1 teaspoon (5 mL) Dijon mustard

½ teaspoon (2 mL) anchovy paste

½ fresh juicy lemon

1 teaspoon (5 mL) red wine vinegar

½ teaspoon (2 mL) Worcestershire sauce

¼ cup (60 mL) extra-virgin olive oil

2 large heads romaine lettuce, torn into bite-size pieces

1½ cups (375 mL) freshly grated Parmesan cheese

1 batch Herbed Croutons (page 159)

Freshly ground black pepper

1. Finely grate the garlic into a large wooden bowl or generous salad bowl. Add the salt and mash to a fine paste using the back of a wooden spoon. Then mash in the mustard and anchovy paste. Squeeze in the lemon juice, then add the red wine vinegar and Worcestershire sauce. Stir rapidly to incorporate into a smooth dressing. Slowly pour in the olive oil, stirring all the while, to make a creamy dressing.

2. Pile the lettuce on top of the dressing and toss with two wooden spoons to coat each and every piece. Sprinkle on the Parmesan and toss again thoroughly. Garnish with Herbed Croutons and freshly ground black pepper.

Herbed Croutons

A few years ago, when all three of my children developed an affinity for Haidi's Caesar Salad (page 156), I took the opportunity to refine my own crouton recipe. Now we love them so much, I make extra for topping soups and salads, storing them in an airtight jar in the freezer until needed. These croutons are delicious as a garnish to my Roasted Tomato and Lentil Soup (page 118) and Tangy Quinoa Carrot Chicken Salad (page 75).

2 small cloves garlic, minced

½ teaspoon (2 mL) sea salt

¼ cup (60 mL) extra-virgin olive oil

2 teaspoons (10 mL) finely minced fresh parsley

1 teaspoon (5 mL) minced fresh thyme

1 teaspoon (5 mL) minced fresh oregano

4 heaping cups (1 L) cubed crusty whole-grain, sourdough or rustic country bread

1. Preheat oven to 350°F (180°C).

2. In a medium bowl, mash together garlic and salt with a fork. Add olive oil and sprinkle in the parsley, thyme and oregano. Stir well to ensure the garlic is evenly distributed.

3. You'll probably want to use your hands for this part. Add the bread cubes and toss with the herbed olive oil until the bread is completely coated and you can't see any dry spots.

4. Spread the bread cubes evenly on a large rimmed baking sheet lined with parchment paper. Bake for 20 to 25 minutes, stirring once, until golden brown. The croutons should feel firm when squeezed, with no give. Turn off oven, leave the door ajar, and cool croutons completely.

5. The croutons will keep in an airtight container at room temperature for up to 3 days or can be frozen for up to 1 month. Recrisp on a baking sheet for a few minutes in a 350°F (180°C) oven.

Tequila-Lime Barbecue Chicken

SERVES 4 TO 6

On a typical summer evening, I am frequently on our back patio, tongs in hand, next to a Weber charcoal grill full of chicken. The children dash about on the grass running races, and occasionally stopping by to try to abscond with a chicken wing. This recipe is so easy, and so well loved, that it's a frequent weeknight dinner all summer long. Paired with another family favourite, Haidi's Caesar Salad (page 156), and a pitcher of Noah's Peach Lemonade (page 169), it's a feast fit for a king.

Ask your butcher to cut a whole chicken into 10 pieces for you, or choose your sharpest knife and hack it up yourself. You'll get better with practice. Keep in mind that this chicken needs plenty of time on the grill to reach its full, tender potential.

1 large chicken (3 to 4 pounds/1.35 to 1.8 kg), cut into 10 pieces

1 teaspoon (5 mL) fine sea salt

½ cup (125 mL) freshly squeezed lime juice

3 tablespoons (45 mL) tequila

2 tablespoons (30 mL) extra-virgin olive oil

2 cloves garlic, minced

1 lime, for serving

1. Preheat grill to at least 400°F (200°C). I prefer charcoal over propane, and build fire on both sides in order to have indirect heat in the middle. Have a spray bottle of water nearby for flare-ups and a sturdy pair of grill tongs.

2. Pat chicken dry with paper towels and season all over with salt. Place chicken skin side down on the hot grill rack. Close the lid and grill chicken until well browned all over, turning as needed, 15 to 20 minutes. Extinguish any flames with the spray bottle.

3. Meanwhile, in a large bowl, whisk together lime juice, tequila, olive oil and garlic. Remove the chicken from the grill and submerge it in the lime marinade. Turn each piece, making sure each one gets coated. Let marinate for about 10 minutes.

4. Reduce grill heat to about 350°F (180°C). Shake off excess marinade and return the chicken to the grill (discard marinade). Continue to cook for another 10 to 15 minutes, until the skin has crisped and the chicken is tender. If you have a meat thermometer, it should register 160°F (70°C) for the breasts and 170°F (75°C) for the thighs.

5. Heap the chicken high on a platter and finish with a squeeze of lime. Get it while it's hot.

Grilled Ratatouille and Sausage Platter

SERVES 4 TO 6

Classic ratatouille is usually stewed, with all the ingredients jumbled together, but I like how a grilled version allows each vegetable to keep its own character and texture. It's also a splendid way to highlight summer produce when feeding a crowd.

Vegetables really don't need much adornment when you cook them at the peak of their growing season. A squeeze of grilled lemon, a drizzle of olive oil and plenty of fresh garden herbs dress this grilled ratatouille, and a cluster of grilled tomatoes self-sauces the whole platter. The directions may look lengthy, but you won't need to rely on the recipe after you've made it the first time.

If you're feeding a hungry crowd, serve with crusty buns and homemade Slow Cooker Tomato Ketchup (page 279) and let your guests assemble an unforgettable summer sandwich.

2 zucchini

2 small eggplants

1 red onion, peeled

2 bell peppers, red, orange or yellow

4 tablespoons (60 mL) extra-virgin olive oil, divided

½ teaspoon (2 mL) fine sea salt, plus more for finishing

6 Toulouse sausage links or your favourite sausage

3 corn cobs, husked and boiled

1 large cluster of medium tomatoes on the vine (6 to 8 tomatoes)

1 lemon, halved

¼ cup (60 mL) loosely packed fresh basil leaves, plus more for garnish

1 tablespoon (15 mL) fresh oregano leaves

1. Preheat grill to 400°F (200°C).

2. Cut the zucchini and eggplants on the diagonal into ½-inch (1 cm) slices. Cut the onion into 8 wedges. Cut the peppers in half, remove the seeds and then quarter the peppers. Combine all these vegetables in a large bowl and toss with 2 tablespoons (30 mL) of the olive oil and the salt.

3. Using a sturdy pair of tongs, transfer the vegetables to the grill and arrange as many as you can in a single layer. You may have to work in batches. Lightly char the vegetables on both sides over direct heat before moving them to cook longer over indirect heat. They will take 7 to 10 minutes, depending on the grill. Leave them a little al dente—they should still have a bit of resistance to the bite.

4. When the vegetables are finished, transfer them to a cutting board. Place the sausages on the grill over direct heat and grill for 2 to 3 minutes, until grill marks appear. Transfer sausages to a spot with indirect heat or lower the grill temperature, and continue grilling, turning frequently to avoid charring, until sausages are cooked through, about 15 minutes.

5. Lightly brush the ears of corn, tomato cluster and lemon halves with olive oil. Place on the grill and keep a close eye on them. Grill for 3 to 4 minutes, turning frequently, until warmed through and they have light grill marks.

6. Roughly chop the grilled vegetables into large pieces and transfer them into a large bowl. Cut the corn off the cob and add it to the vegetables. Squeeze both halves of the grilled lemon over the vegetables. Drizzle in the remaining 2 tablespoons (30 mL) olive oil and add a pinch of salt. Tear basil and oregano into shreds and sprinkle over the top. Toss the vegetables gently to coat with the dressing.

7. Heap the grilled ratatouille onto a large serving platter. Top with sausages and grilled tomatoes. Garnish with additional fresh basil and serve warm.

Cumin-Rubbed Pork Tenderloin
with Zesty Mojo Sauce

It seems I am always feeding a crowd on summer weekends, and this is one recipe I keep in my back pocket for a quick grilled meal. The mild, lean pork pairs well with the bold citrus and garlic of the zesty mojo sauce—and everything about this dish pairs well with a pitcher of margaritas!

Both the tenderloin and the sauce are better when marinated in advance, making this dish ideal for entertaining. Serve the grilled tenderloin straight off the grill, or slice and serve cold in a sandwich with a side of homemade Baby Dill Pickles (page 270).

3 teaspoons (15 mL) ground cumin, divided

1 teaspoon (5 mL) ground cinnamon, divided

1 teaspoon (5 mL) sweet paprika

½ teaspoon (2 mL) freshly ground black pepper

1½ teaspoons (7 mL) sea salt, divided

3 pork tenderloins

Zest and juice of 3 medium oranges

Zest and juice of 3 limes

1 clove garlic, finely minced

⅓ cup (75 mL) extra-virgin olive oil

Fresh cilantro, for garnish

1. In a small bowl, stir together 2 teaspoons (10 mL) of the cumin, ½ teaspoon (2 mL) of the cinnamon, the paprika, pepper and 1 teaspoon (5 mL) of the salt. Rub all over the tenderloins. Place pork in a resealable bag and marinate, refrigerated, for 4 to 8 hours.

2. Meanwhile, in a small bowl, combine the zest and juice from the oranges and limes. Add the minced garlic and the remaining 1 teaspoon (5 mL) cumin, ½ teaspoon (2 mL) cinnamon and ½ teaspoon (2 mL) salt. Pour in the olive oil and whisk to combine. Cover and refrigerate for 4 to 8 hours.

3. Preheat grill to 400°F (200°C) and prepare the coals for direct cooking.

4. Remove the tenderloins from the resealable bag and discard marinade. Grill the tenderloins, with the lid closed as much as possible, for 15 to 20 minutes, rotating every 5 minutes for even grilling. Toward the end, baste with the mojo sauce. Remove from the grill when the internal temperature reaches 150°F (65°C). Brush generously with mojo sauce and let rest for 5 minutes. Slice into ½-inch (1 cm) rounds, garnish with torn fresh cilantro, and serve with remaining mojo sauce.

Bloody Caesars

SERVES 2

≫

The Bloody Caesar is the sassier sister to the Bloody Mary, containing clam juice in addition to the familiar tomato juice, spices and celery garnish. Don't knock it until you try it; the Bloody Caesar is Canada's most consumed cocktail. I've been known to mix up a pitcher for a New Year's brunch, but my favourite time of the year to serve an ice-cold Caesar is in the height of summer, when produce is fresh. The garnish comes straight from my garden—baby carrots, cherry tomatoes, radishes and pea pods—and I occasionally make my own tomato juice when I have them in abundance.

I encourage you to make this recipe your own. It should be customized according to taste—and everyone takes his or her Bloody Caesar a little differently. Some love a triple hit of hot sauce, while others prefer more lime juice. Others appreciate vodka, and some take their cocktail with no alcohol at all. I make mine with tequila blanco and no apologies. Don't leave out the garnish and remember to have fun with it.

2 teaspoons (10 mL) celery salt

Freshly ground black pepper

2 wedges of lime

2 cups (500 mL) ice

2 ounces (60 mL) tequila blanco

2 tablespoons (30 mL) freshly squeezed lime juice

½ teaspoon (2 mL) agave syrup

½ teaspoon (2 mL) red wine vinegar

½ teaspoon (2 mL) Worcestershire sauce

Dash of hot sauce

1½ cups (300 mL) tomato juice, chilled

½ cup (125 mL) clam juice, chilled

2 leafy celery stalks, for garnish

Optional garnishes: Pickled Fiddleheads (page 266), Baby Dill Pickles (page 270), radishes or cherry tomatoes

1. Place the celery salt in a shallow dish and add a crack of black pepper. Rub the rims of two 1-pint (500 mL) glasses or mason jars with the lime wedges. Dip the rims in the salt and pepper. Fill each glass with about 1 cup (250 mL) of ice.

2. In a cocktail shaker, combine tequila, lime juice, agave, red wine vinegar, Worcestershire sauce, hot sauce, tomato juice and clam juice. Shake very well. Divide the cocktail between the two glasses, pouring over the ice.

3. Add a stalk of celery to each glass, and any other garnish you desire. Serve at once.

Noah's Peach Lemonade

Lemonade has always been my boys' number one request for birthday sips. It's always made from scratch, and since lemons aren't exactly local, it's a special treat. I taught my children to make the lemonade themselves, and Noah credits himself with "inventing" the addition of peaches. In this fruity version, we infuse a honey simple syrup with sweet Ontario peaches, and then marry it with tart lemon zest and juice. Light and bright, thirst-quenching and delicious, this vibrant drink is the right sip for summer.

Don't toss out the stewed peaches after you strain the syrup. They're delicious with yogurt for breakfast.

1½ cups (375 mL) liquid honey	Zest of 4 lemons	4 cups (1 L) ice
4 cups (1 L) water	1 cup (250 mL) freshly squeezed lemon juice (about 4 large lemons)	Thinly sliced lemons and peaches, for garnish
6 cups (1.5 L) chopped peaches (about 8 medium)		

1. Combine honey and water in a large pot and bring to a simmer over high heat. Stir until honey is dissolved.

2. Add peaches and lemon zest. Reduce heat to medium-low and simmer for 5 minutes. Turn off heat and allow infusion to cool completely.

3. Strain through a fine-mesh sieve into a large pitcher or jar. Stir lemon juice into the peach simple syrup; this is now your lemonade concentrate. Chill until ready to serve.

4. To serve, mix peach lemonade concentrate with water to taste. Pour into a serving pitcher or jar and top up with ice. Add a garnish of thinly sliced lemons and peaches and serve at once.

Strawberry Rhubarb Pie

SERVES 6 TO 8

In Quebec, the season for strawberries and rhubarb begins in late May and stretches through until August, thanks to my prolific rhubarb patch and the late-summer berry varieties of our local farmers. During that stretch, I bake many double-crust pies in my kitchen, stuffed to bursting with this winning combination of seasonal fruits. Some pies I bake right away and others I freeze unbaked for another day. To bake from frozen, just add a good 20 minutes to the baking time.

Since the berries are in their prime and very sweet, there is no need for an excess of sugar in the recipe and the flavours of the fruit really shine through. Pure vanilla bean is a luxurious flavouring that sets this pie apart from all others. The beans can be found at gourmet grocers, and it is well worth buying a few to store in the pantry. While vanilla will always be my favourite addition, you can also add a little grated ginger, a few pinches of ground cardamom or a teaspoon of fresh lemon zest. I can assure you your guests would be happy with any of these variations so long as they arrive in the form of a strawberry rhubarb pie.

1 recipe Flaky Pie Pastry (page 251)	Seeds scraped from 1 vanilla bean	3 cups (750 mL) sliced rhubarb (about ¼ inch/5 mm thick)
¾ cup (175 mL) raw cane sugar, plus more for topping	3 tablespoons (45 mL) instant tapioca	3 cups (750 mL) packed sliced strawberries
	1 tablespoon (15 mL) cornstarch	1 egg, beaten, for glaze

1. Preheat oven to 425°F (220°C). Roll out one half of the Flaky Pie Pastry, following the instructions on page 251, and line a 9-inch (23 cm) pie plate; chill. Roll out the top crust, slide it onto a parchment-lined cookie sheet, and chill.

2. Pour the sugar into a large bowl. Use your fingertips to massage the vanilla seeds into the sugar until it is thoroughly distributed. Stir in tapioca and cornstarch. Tumble in the sliced rhubarb and strawberries and gently toss with a spatula until the fruit is well coated.

3. Heap half of the filling into the pie shell. Spread it around evenly and pack it down firmly with the palm of your hand. Heap the remaining fruit on top and arrange evenly.

(recipe continues)

4. Brush the pastry rim with the beaten egg. Carefully transfer the chilled top crust onto the pie. Press down gently around the edges to seal the top and bottom crust together. Trim the edge leaving about 1-inch (2.5 cm) overhang, then fold it under and crimp it all the way around. Brush the top crust lightly with the beaten egg. Sprinkle with a little cane sugar and cut 6 steam vents.

5. Place the pie on a rimmed baking sheet and bake for 15 minutes. Reduce the oven temperature to 375°F (190°C) and bake for 50 to 60 minutes longer. The crust should be a deep golden and the filling will bubble up through the steam vents. Transfer the pie to a wire rack and let stand for at least 30 minutes before cutting. For best leak-free filling results, allow to cool completely before serving.

TIP: *For the best filling consistency, I have found a combination of cornstarch and instant tapioca to be the absolute best. Instant tapioca is powdered and flavourless, and it disappears completely into the filling. In a pinch you could use pearl tapioca and grind it into a powder yourself. You could also use all cornstarch, but it will leave the filling looking a bit murky and tasting slightly chalky.*

Apple Almond Galette

SERVES 8

How I managed to get hired as a pastry chef at a tiny French bistro long ago is beyond me. By the end of the first day, it was painfully clear I was in over my head. The only way I kept my job was that the chef, a young fellow direct from France, was sweet on me. Along with génoise, crème brûlée and mousse au chocolat, he taught me the art of a classic French apple tart. It was a simple but decadent dessert, with almond frangipane and artfully arranged apple slices.

Nowadays, I bake my own version of that frangipane tart; it's often my go-to dessert for family dinners when I've volunteered to bring something sweet. I keep 1-pound (450 g) packages of puff pastry in my freezer and I always have a drawer of apples in my crisper. The frangipane freezes well, too, so I often make a double batch and tuck away half for another time. Eventually the Frenchman stopped watching over my shoulder as I worked, but he never stopped proposing marriage for as long as I stayed on at the bistro.

1 pound (450 g) puff pastry, thawed overnight in the refrigerator

⅓ cup (75 mL) unsalted butter, softened

⅔ cup (150 mL) raw cane sugar, divided, plus 1 tablespoon (15 mL) for sprinkling

2 medium eggs

½ cup (125 mL) ground almonds

2 tablespoons (30 mL) all-purpose flour

4 large Granny Smith or Russet apples

¼ teaspoon (1 mL) freshly grated nutmeg

1 tablespoon (15 mL) unsalted butter, melted

2 tablespoons (30 mL) sliced almonds, for granish

1. Preheat oven to 400°F (200°C). Line a rimmed baking sheet with parchment paper.

2. On a lightly floured counter, roll puff pastry into a roughly 11- × 16-inch (28 × 40 cm) rectangle approximately ⅛ inch (3 mm) thick. Transfer to the baking sheet and place in the freezer while you prepare the filling.

3. In a medium bowl, cream together the softened butter and ⅓ cup (75 mL) of the sugar. Add 1 egg and beat until smooth. Stir in the ground almonds and flour until a smooth paste forms. This frangipane may be made up to 3 days in advance and stored in the refrigerator.

4. Peel and core the apples, then cut into quarters and slice into ¼-inch (5 mm) wedges. Tumble the apples into a medium bowl and toss with another ⅓ cup (75 mL) sugar and the nutmeg.

(recipe continues)

5.   Spread the almond frangipane over the puff pastry, leaving at least a 3-inch (8 cm) border on all sides. Arrange the apple slices over the frangipane, overlapping and tucking them in close together.

6.   Fold the sides of the puff pastry up and over the apples in an easy, free-form way, making an edge of at least 2 inches (5 cm). The beauty of a galette is that it doesn't have to look perfect. Pinch the pastry folds firmly together to seal them.

7.   Brush the apples with the melted butter. Lightly beat the remaining egg and brush it over the puff pastry. Sprinkle everything with the remaining 1 tablespoon (15 mL) sugar. Bake for 50 to 55 minutes, until the pastry is golden and the apples are soft when poked with a fork. Cool slightly, then sprinkle with sliced almonds and serve warm. The galette is best enjoyed on the same day it is made.

Winter Squash Pie

Maple-sweetened and lightly spiced, this autumnal pie never lasts long in my house because it is a favourite of all three children. We eat it slightly chilled, our slices heaped high with whipped cream. I've been making my pumpkin-style pies with roasted winter squash ever since I was twelve years old and read that they were far more flavourful than basic pumpkin. And they are! I think butternut is the best, but kabocha or Hubbard also work well. The maple syrup complements the squash and is another variant to the classic that I adopted when I moved to Quebec.

Don't be daunted by roasting your own squash. Simply cut the squash in half, remove seeds and roast until soft. Then scoop out the flesh and purée it until smooth. That's it! In a pinch you could use canned pumpkin purée, but it won't have the depth of flavour that a roasted squash will give.

½ recipe Flaky Pie Pastry (page 251)

4 medium eggs

Seeds scraped from 1 vanilla bean (or 2 teaspoons/10 mL pure vanilla extract)

1 tablespoon (15 mL) Autumn Spice Blend (page 244)

¾ teaspoon (4 mL) sea salt

1¼ cups (300 mL) winter squash purée

⅔ cup (150 mL) pure maple syrup

1 cup (250 mL) heavy (35%) cream

Sweetened whipped cream, for garnish

1. Preheat oven to 375°F (190°C). Roll out the Flaky Pie Pastry, following the instructions on page 251, and line a 9-inch (23 cm) pie plate; chill while you mix up the filling.

2. In a large bowl, whisk the eggs until frothy. Tip in the vanilla seeds, Autumn Spice Blend and salt, then whisk together until well blended. Add the squash purée and maple syrup and again whisk well. Finally, stir in the cream.

3. Place the pie shell on the middle rack of the oven. Slide the rack out a couple of inches and pour the filling into the pie shell. Slowly slide the oven rack back in place, taking care not to spill the filling. (If you find yourself with a little extra filling, simply pour it into a couple of ramekins and bake them alongside your pie until they are set.)

4. Bake for 50 to 60 minutes, rotating the pie after about 30 minutes to ensure even browning of the crust. When the centre of the pie jiggles only slightly when the pan is moved, the pie is ready. Cool on a wire rack. When the pie is room temperature, cover with plastic wrap and refrigerate until ready to serve. Pie will keep, covered in the fridge, for up to 3 days, or wrap well and freeze for up to 8 weeks.

HOMEMADE HOSPITALITY: THROW AN OLD-FASHIONED PIE SOCIAL

You never need an excuse for pie, or for bringing people together to share pie. So how about hosting an old-fashioned pie social—basically a fancy term for an all-pie potluck. How do you do this? Well, one of my longest-running strategies for entertaining large groups has been to delegate the dessert to guests. In this case, obviously, dessert is the main event, which means you're in charge of providing drinks. As long as your guests don't mind being "limited" to making pie, you're all set.

My last pie social took place in the height of summer, in a shady corner of my backyard, while the kids ran around and nearly eighty guests mingled together over iced drinks. It was one for the books: Strawberry Rhubarb (page 171), maple pecan, avocado Key lime, mocha cream, blueberry mascarpone, chocolate caramel, lemon chiffon, Apple Almond Galette (page 173), pumpkin spice … That's just a sampling of the *sixteen* delicious pies that my extended family and I baked for the occasion. It is certainly going to have to be an annual event.

So you've picked a date for your pie social. Now to make plans. Inviting bakers to bring their homemade pies is what puts the "social" into an event like this one. Of course, anyone can (and should!) bring a pie. Remember, there is no such thing as a bad homemade pie; every one has a redeeming quality.

Don't be tempted to assign specific pies to your bakers; no two pies are ever going to be exactly the same because no two bakers are exactly the same. However, be ready to offer suggestions and a well-tested recipe if one of your bakers can't decide what to make.

Do remember the classics, because they really can't be beat. Even if they have been done over and over for decades, traditional pies such as apple, pecan and blueberry deserve a spot at the pie social.

Display each pie on a pedestal if possible, thus giving it its own spotlight. Whether you use an overturned cake pan, a tin picnic box or a wooden trivet, a little height adds a great visual appeal to your table arrangement.

I like to cut my pies into very small slices—sixteen or even twenty—so that guests can sample a wide selection without filling up too quickly. Enlist a few helpers, equipped with serrated knives, because cutting and serving takes a while. Then set out plates, forks and napkins and let the party begin!

There is no wrong season to make and share pie, meaning this event isn't limited to lazy summer evenings. Your gathering could be with extended family around Thanksgiving, with pecan tarts and cranberry galettes. There could be hot spiced cider to accompany the pie, and after the feasting, everyone could take a long walk in the fall leaves.

Perhaps a winter holiday would be best suited to your pie social. Imagine warm Apple Almond Galette (page 173) and a whipped cream–topped chocolate peppermint pie served up around the Christmas tree. A time to put the kids to bed and savour something decidedly grown-up like my maple-sweetened Winter Squash Pie (page 177).

My Strawberry Rhubarb Pie (page 171) has been a Father's Day tradition for a few years now. Our local berries arrive in June, and by the third Sunday in the month, I've paired them with my own rhubarb in a bevy of pies that are consumed down to the last crumb.

Really, any season can be pie season.

Everyday Suppers

I've recently passed the ten-year milestone of cooking dinner for my family nearly every night. While that might sound tedious to some of you, I embrace the challenge of preparing nourishing food that the whole family loves and keeping it creative and interesting. Most days, anyway.

Family dinner is a tradition I have staunchly held on to, long before it was trendy and recommended by the experts. It started with a little blond toddler who threw his food under the high chair night after night, much to my frustration. I learned to do my best and then let go of the rest when it came to feeding my youngsters. And it's a lesson I am revisiting now as they transition into tweens.

Over the years I came to understand that time together around the table is crucial to building a healthy family food culture. My husband Danny and I were both raised in homes that emphasized the importance of family dinner, but today it means much more to us than tradition.

If we examine our average day, minute by minute, that dinnertime hour is often the longest time during the week the five of us are gathered face to face. It's a time to listen and to be heard. A time to reminisce and to make plans.

But this commitment to family dinner is not without its rocky moments. The truth is, the family table is a wonderfully intimate yet ever so imperfect gathering place. On a nightly basis we're dealing with spilled milk, tossed food, stormy attitudes and questionable manners. Some nights it would be a lot easier to serve peanut butter sandwiches on paper plates to the kids and then, after we tuck them into bed, sit down to a hot! spicy! uninterrupted! meal (and, on rare occasions, this *does* happen), but we're committed to having dinner as a family.

Experts say if you uphold the family dinner hour, your kids will be less likely to suffer from depression or substance abuse, while enjoying higher self-esteem and better grades. That is both utterly astonishing and absolutely believable.

The benefits continue to add up. Preparing a meal from scratch for your family is one of the most rewarding actions you can take for healthy kids. The nourishing foods they learn to enjoy now will shape their palates to appreciate unprocessed foods, and the meals will meld together to become their fond food memories.

And I'd better throw this in, too—the act of gathering is far more important than what's on the plate. Sure, aim for wholesome, balanced meals as often as you can, but avoid having standards set so high that you might throw in the towel before scrambling a platter of eggs for dinner.

Every family will have a different approach to dinner and it's up to you to find your own way of making it work best. Are you a planner or more of a last-minute, make-it-on-the-fly sort of cook? Play to your strengths in the kitchen, and remember that the end result isn't perfection, it is honest, home-style family food. Here are just a few dinner ideas, broken down to suit your meal styles and the time you have available.

- SLOW COOKER SOLUTIONS Slow Cooker Carnitas (page 202), Mild Chicken and Chickpea Curry (page 205), Slow Cooker Root Vegetable Cider Stew (page 131)
- MAKE-AHEAD MEALS Skillet Zucchini-Chicken Parmesan (page 196), Braised Lamb with Olives and Tomatoes (page 211), Spinach Lasagna Stuffed Sweet Peppers (page 117), Gardener's Sloppy Joes (page 114)
- SUPER-FAST FOOD Coriander-Crusted Salmon with Parsnip Fries (page 193), Quick Crustless Ham and Cheese Quiche (page 206), Tofu Vegetable Stir-Fry with Cashews (page 121)
- ALL HANDS ON DECK Every-Season Risotto (page 189), One-Pot Shrimp and Pea Orzo (page 195), Vietnamese Summer Rolls (page 110)
- ONE-POT WONDERS Roast Chicken with Bay Leaf and Barley (page 199), Cranberry-Glazed Turkey Meatloaf with Baked Sweet Potatoes (page 201)

OVEN-TO-TABLE COOKWARE

Danny and I inherited an old stoneware bean pot from his mother, the likes of which can be found in antique shops across Quebec. This brown pot with a small round lid has simmered countless batches of maple-baked beans and served them up at the table in rustic style. It is this oven-to-table food presentation that I embrace wholeheartedly.

Oven-to-table cookware saves time and effort spent on meals. Whether your preference is stoneware, enamelware or vintage Pyrex, there is sure to be a collection of cookware and bakeware pretty enough for your dinner table. You'll still need a salad bowl and a bread basket, but there's no reason why the main and side dishes can't be served up straight from the oven.

Here's a lineup of the oven-to-table cookware in my kitchen that I reach for every day.

ENAMELWARE

Shatterproof, naturally nonstick, lightweight and dishwasher safe, it's hard to beat enamelware for oven-to-table serving. These pans are great for outdoor entertaining, especially around a campfire. Although I love my mismatched vintage collection, British kitchenware company Falcon Enamelware makes some beautiful sets (falconenamelware.com). See Roast Chicken with Bay Leaf and Barley (page 199).

COPPER SKILLET OR BRAISER

A low, two-handled skillet is ideal for frittatas, sauces and even desserts like cobblers and crisps. Mine was a hand-me-down and is still just as good as new. See Skillet Zucchini-Chicken Parmesan (page 196).

ENAMELLED CAST IRON

Formidable, dependable and beautiful. Every kitchen should have one sturdy enamelled cast-iron pan for hearty dinners.

The biggest appeal of enamelled cast-iron casserole dishes is their stovetop-to-oven-to-table abilities. For making gravy, there's nothing better: while the roast rests, the pan can go over the flame to loosen all the tasty caramelized bits stuck to the bottom. See Lentil Cottage Pie with Rutabaga Mash (page 123).

FRENCH OR DUTCH OVEN

No matter the size, the French oven (or Dutch oven) is both highly versatile and durable. With a lid in a slow oven, it acts as a slow cooker, yet you can also boil pasta in it and much more. They come in a range of beautiful colours and last a lifetime. I have two, and they are frequently the centrepiece of our dinner table. See Every-Season Risotto (page 189).

PYREX

For a perfectly browned bottom pie crust, there's nothing better than a Pyrex pie plate. There has probably been a piece or two of this classic bakeware in every kitchen in North America for a few generations. Now the antique casseroles with soft colours and pretty patterns are fetching high prices on eBay with vintage lovers.

I haven't started my vintage Pyrex collection yet (although I'm partial to the Turquoise Snowflake set), but I have a few curated pieces that frequently appear on the dinner table. See Mild Chicken and Chickpea Curry (page 205).

CERAMIC BAKER

This pan can't go on the stovetop, but it still fits the oven-to-table description. It's invaluable for gratins, casseroles, lasagnas, quiches and baked desserts. I love my square blue Le Creuset that comes with a lid, but they come in all shapes and sizes. See Roasted Garlic Scalloped Potatoes (page 217).

Every-Season Risotto

At some point in my parenting journey, I discovered that risotto was an indispensable vehicle for getting my children to eat vegetables. Ever since, I've seldom been without the basic ingredients for risotto: chicken or vegetable stock in the freezer, butter and Parmesan in the fridge, rice and onions in the pantry.

This is my basic easy-to-make recipe, the beginning of a meal that celebrates the seasons. To this everyday risotto I might add cubes of roasted squash, fresh English peas or finely shaved baby zucchini. It is a carrier for slow-roasted cherry tomatoes, asparagus shoots, wild mushrooms and sweet corn kernels. In short, the only limit is your palate. Enjoy with a salad, such as Haidi's Caesar Salad (page 156).

6 cups (1.5 L) Basic Vegetable Stock (page 231)

Pinch of saffron threads

3 tablespoons (45 mL) salted butter, divided

1 tablespoon (15 mL) extra-virgin olive oil

1 medium red onion, diced

1½ cups (375 mL) Arborio rice

⅓ cup (75 mL) dry white wine or dry vermouth

1¼ cups (300 mL) freshly grated Parmesan cheese, divided

½ teaspoon (2 mL) freshly ground white or black pepper

Salt

1. In a medium pot, bring Basic Vegetable Stock to a boil, then reduce heat and keep warm. Drop in the saffron threads, which will colour it slightly yellow.

2. In a large, heavy saucepan over medium heat, melt 1 tablespoon (15 mL) of the butter with the olive oil. When the butter is bubbling, add the onion and stir with a sturdy wooden spoon. Cook the onion for about 5 minutes, until it is soft and translucent.

3. Add rice all at once and stir thoroughly. You want the rice to be completely coated in butter and give each grain a chance to be toasted. This takes about 1 minute. Add the white wine—be careful, as it will steam viciously—and stir well. Cook for another minute, until most of the liquid is absorbed.

(recipe continues)

4.   Add several ladles of hot stock to the rice and stir well. Continue stirring frequently until most of the stock is absorbed. Continue adding stock a ladle at a time, stirring often until each addition is absorbed before adding more, for about 15 minutes. You may need more liquid, in which case, just add hot water. Taste occasionally—you want the rice to be tender but still have a slight bite and the risotto to be creamy. If you are adding any cooked vegetables, now is the time.

5.   Tip in 1 cup (250 mL) of the Parmesan, the pepper and the remaining 2 tablespoons (30 mL) butter. Stir to combine, but don't over-stir or the risotto will become gummy instead of creamy. Taste the risotto and add salt as needed.

6.   Transfer the risotto to a serving bowl or plates and top with the remaining ¼ cup (60 mL) Parmesan. Serve at once.

> TIP: *Be sure to taste the risotto for salt after you add the Parmesan and butter. Depending on the volume of vegetables you add, you may need to use a generous amount of salt. Adding a pinch at a time between each tasting can make the difference between an okay risotto and an excellent risotto.*

Coriander-Crusted Salmon with Parsnip Fries

SERVES 4

All of my children love fish, and as it is such an important part of a healthy diet, I try to keep salmon on regular dinner rotation. I also aim for a nutritious meal by using parsnips for the baked fries, although you could use a combination of both parsnip and potato.

This is one of our quick dinners, even if it doesn't look anything like typical fast food. Cutting the parsnips and mixing the spice blend ahead of time makes for an easy meal at dinnertime.

Look for wild-caught or organic farmed salmon when you shop, and don't be shy about asking your fishmonger about the source and the freshness of the product.

1 pound (450 g) parsnips, peeled

2 tablespoons (30 mL) extra-virgin olive oil, divided

1 tablespoon (15 mL) coriander seeds, crushed

½ teaspoon (2 mL) freshly ground black pepper

1 teaspoon (5 mL) fine sea salt

1 tablespoon (15 mL) grainy mustard

1 tablespoon (15 mL) liquid honey

4 medium skin-on wild sockeye salmon fillets

1. Position oven racks in the upper and lower thirds of the oven and preheat oven to 425°F (220°C).

2. Cut the parsnips lengthwise into strips ½ inch (1 cm) thick and then cut into french fry shapes. Don't worry if they are not uniform. Tumble parsnips into a large bowl and drizzle with 1 tablespoon of the olive oil. Toss them with a pair of tongs until they are completely coated in oil; this helps them to get crispy.

3. In a small bowl, stir together the crushed coriander seeds, pepper and salt. Sprinkle half the spice mix over the parsnips and toss to coat. Spread parsnips in a single layer on a rimmed baking sheet. Roast on the upper rack, stirring and turning once, for 15 to 20 minutes until golden and crispy on the edges.

4. Meanwhile, stir together the mustard and honey. Brush on the tops of the salmon fillets (not the skin side). Crust the salmon with the remaining spice mix.

5. Heat the remaining 1 tablespoon (15 mL) of olive oil in a large oven-safe skillet over medium-high heat. Sear salmon, spice side down, for 2 minutes. Gently turn the fish. Transfer the pan to the oven, below the fries, and roast for 7 to 9 minutes, until fish feels firm to the touch and is a light pink throughout.

6. Delicately transfer the salmon to plates or a platter and heap the parsnip fries around the fish. Finish the fries with a sprinkling of salt and serve immediately with Slow Cooker Tomato Ketchup (page 279).

One-Pot Shrimp and Pea Orzo

SERVES 4

Garlic butter fans, unite! This one-pot wonder might look like it has a daunting list of ingredients, but they are mostly spices, and they add up to the most flavourful bowl of comfort food you can imagine.

You could ramp up the cayenne if you like things on the spicy side, or double the butter for an extra-creamy special-occasion version. Be sure to have all your ingredients ready to go, because the cooking time is quite short. Then serve at once with crusty bread and more white wine and call it a day.

2 teaspoons (10 mL) sweet paprika

1 teaspoon (5 mL) dried oregano

½ teaspoon (2 mL) dried thyme

½ teaspoon (2 mL) fine sea salt

½ teaspoon (2 mL) freshly ground black pepper

Dash of cayenne pepper

2 cups (500 mL) orzo

1¼ cups (300 mL) Basic Vegetable Stock (page 231)

¼ cup (60 mL) dry white wine

5 green onions, sliced

2 cloves garlic, finely chopped

1 cup (250 mL) frozen peas

3 tablespoons (45 mL) salted butter, cubed

12 ounces (340 g) cold-water shrimp, peeled and deveined

Zest and juice of 1 lemon

1. In a small bowl, stir together paprika, oregano, thyme, salt, black pepper and cayenne.

2. Bring a large pot of water to a boil and salt it generously. Cook orzo according to package directions, draining it when it is still a little al dente. Set aside.

3. Combine the Basic Vegetable Stock and white wine in the same pot. Add the spice mix and bring to a boil. Add the green onions, garlic and peas. Return to a rapid boil. Drop in the butter cubes and stir until the butter is melted.

4. Carefully add the shrimp and cook for 2 minutes, or until shrimp turn pink. Add the cooked orzo and the lemon zest and juice. Stir for a minute or two until the pasta absorbs all the flavourful liquid. Serve immediately.

TIP: *It's best not to purchase shrimp that comes from Asia. All you have to do is Google "shrimp slavery" to know what I am talking about. Either look for something from our North American fisheries or don't eat shrimp at all.*

There are plenty of great options for Atlantic or Pacific Northwest wild-caught shrimp, also known as cold-water shrimp. There are many different species, but both Atlantic and Pacific Northwest shrimp can be marketed as "northern" or "pink" shrimp, so check labels carefully or ask your fishmonger where they came from.

Skillet Zucchini-Chicken Parmesan

SERVES 6

❧

We're a family who loves our comfort foods, so I am always looking for ways to incorporate vegetables into the classics. This twist on chicken Parmesan uses a little less meat and includes rounds of zucchini under the traditional bubbly tomato sauce and melted cheese.

This is one of my favourite dishes to take to new parents, as it is so nourishing and comforting. I serve this over pasta to my crew, but it would be delicious on its own as a gluten-free main dish.

1 teaspoon (5 mL) dried oregano

½ teaspoon (2 mL) ground savory

1 teaspoon (5 mL) fine sea salt

¼ teaspoon (2 mL) freshly ground black pepper

3 boneless, skinless chicken breasts

2 teaspoons (10 mL) extra-virgin olive oil

¼ cup (60 mL) freshly grated Parmesan cheese

2½ cups (625 mL) tomato sauce

1 medium zucchini, sliced ¼ inch (5 mm) thick

6 slices fresh mozzarella cheese (about ½ inch/1 cm thick)

1 pound (450 g) spaghetti

Chopped fresh oregano or parsley, for garnish

1. In a small bowl, stir together the oregano, savory, salt and pepper.

2. Cut chicken breasts in half lengthwise so that you have 6 pieces. Cover chicken with plastic wrap and pound the thickest parts of the chicken with a rolling pin or meat tenderizer. The pieces should be no thicker than 1 inch (2.5 cm). Remove the plastic wrap and season the chicken all over with the herb blend.

3. In a large braiser or lidded skillet, heat the olive oil over medium-high heat. Working in batches, sear chicken until lightly golden, 2 to 4 minutes per side. Reduce heat to medium-low. Evenly sprinkle the Parmesan over the chicken. Pour the tomato sauce over and around the chicken. Cover the pan and simmer for 15 minutes.

4. Add the zucchini to the pan, tucking the pieces around the chicken. Partially cover and simmer for 15 minutes more. Top each piece of chicken with a slice of fresh mozzarella. Replace the lid and finish cooking the dish for about 10 minutes, until the mozzarella melts. Cool slightly while you prepare the pasta.

5. Bring a large pot of salted water to a boil. Cook the spaghetti according to the package directions. Drain well and transfer to a large serving bowl. Serve the zucchini-chicken parmesan over the spaghetti, garnished with fresh oregano or parsley.

Roast Chicken with Bay Leaf and Barley

SERVES 4 TO 6

This best-loved chicken dinner never fails to make the house smell intoxicating. During the roasting time, the barley becomes soft and risotto-like while the chicken skin crisps up nicely. It's the best of both worlds: a braise and a roast. Don't skip the resting time; the drippings from the chicken are the finishing touch to the dish.

Spatchcocked simply means a split and flattened whole chicken. Ask your butcher to do this for you, or do it yourself. Use a sharp, sturdy knife or kitchen shears, and cut down the backbone on both sides to remove it entirely. Open the chicken, lay it on a cutting board skin side up and press gently between the breasts to flatten the bird.

1 teaspoon (5 mL) extra-virgin olive oil

1 cup (250 mL) pearl barley

1 small leek, white and pale green part only, washed and chopped

½ teaspoon (2 mL) sea salt, divided

⅓ cup (75 mL) dry white wine

2⅔ cups (650 mL) water

1 small organic chicken (about 4 pounds/1.8 kg), spatchcocked

¼ teaspoon (1 mL) freshly ground black pepper

5 dried bay leaves

Cranberry Compote with Port and Pepper (page 282), for serving

1. Preheat oven to 400°F (200°C). Brush a 13- × 9-inch (3.5 L) roasting pan with the olive oil.

2. Sprinkle the barley evenly in the pan. Top with chopped leeks and a sprinkling of salt. Pour the white wine and water over the barley.

3. Trim excess fat from the chicken. Place the chicken skin side up on the barley. Season the chicken with the remaining salt and the pepper. Tuck a bay leaf under the skin of each thigh and each breast. Nestle the remaining bay leaf in the barley.

4. Cover the pan tightly with foil and bake for 45 minutes. Remove the foil and roast for an additional 45 minutes, until the liquid is reduced and the chicken is lightly browned. Remove from the oven and cover loosely with foil again. Let chicken rest for 10 minutes. Serve with Cranberry Compote with Port and Pepper.

Cranberry-Glazed Turkey Meatloaf with Baked Sweet Potatoes

SERVES 4 TO 6

This sheet-pan supper is reminiscent of Christmas dinner, with its sage- and savory-scented cranberry-glazed turkey and fluffy sweet potato side. Fortunately, it comes together quickly. Wrapping the sweet potatoes in foil is the secret to cooking them alongside the meatloaf. They bake quickly and remain moist, needing nothing more than a finishing dab of butter on top.

Turkey meatloaf

2 pounds (900 g) ground turkey

1 large egg, lightly beaten

½ medium sweet onion, finely diced

½ cup (125 mL) panko crumbs

1 teaspoon (5 mL) grainy mustard

1 teaspoon (5 mL) minced fresh sage

½ teaspoon (2 mL) ground savory

¾ teaspoon (4 mL) fine sea salt

¼ teaspoon (1 mL) freshly ground black pepper

2 tablespoons (30 mL) chicken stock

4 to 6 small sweet potatoes

Cranberry sauce

2 cups (500 mL) fresh or frozen cranberries

¾ cup (175 mL) freshly squeezed orange juice

3 tablespoons (45 mL) pure maple syrup

1 teaspoon (5 mL) grainy mustard

1. Preheat oven to 375°F (190°C). Brush a large rimmed baking sheet lightly with olive oil.

2. MAKE THE TURKEY MEATLOAF Place the ground turkey in a large bowl and add the egg, onion, panko, mustard, sage, savory, salt, pepper and chicken stock. Using your hands, gently but thoroughly combine the ingredients with as little work as possible. Heap the turkey onto the baking sheet and shape it into a free-form football-shaped loaf.

3. Wrap each sweet potato in foil and arrange around the meatloaf. Place the pan in the oven and bake for 45 minutes.

4. MAKE THE CRANBERRY SAUCE While the meatloaf bakes, in a medium saucepan, combine cranberries, orange juice, maple syrup and mustard. Bring to a boil over medium-high heat, then reduce heat to low and simmer, stirring often, for 10 minutes. Remove from heat and crush the berries with the back of a fork.

5. After the meatloaf has been baking for 45 minutes, brush on about ½ cup (125 mL) of the Cranberry Sauce. Return to the oven for a final 15 minutes or until the internal temperature reaches 160°F (70°C). Let rest for 10 minutes. Check sweet potatoes for doneness and cook for longer if needed.

6. Unwrap sweet potatoes, slice turkey meatloaf and serve both with Cranberry Sauce.

Slow Cooker Carnitas

SERVES 4 · REQUIRES TIME FOR PREP

Shredded chicken gets a bit boring in soft-shell tacos, so we like to switch things up with a pork shoulder braised in lime juice, garlic and cumin. It's juicy and flavourful thanks to a long, slow cook, and shreds nicely for tortillas.

Here's a meal the whole family can help get on the table. Enlist little hands to prep lettuce, fry tortillas or stem cilantro. Our toppings vary with the seasons, but homemade Summertime Salsa (page 277) and plenty of lettuce are constants.

You'll likely want to think ahead and make a double recipe of the pork; it reheats well from frozen as long as you package it in a portion of the cooking liquid. A freezer stash of carnitas pork and a bag of corn tortillas ensures a quick dinner down the road.

2 pounds (900 g) skinless, boneless pork shoulder roast

1 teaspoon (5 mL) freshly ground cumin

1 teaspoon (5 mL) fine sea salt

½ teaspoon (2 mL) freshly ground black pepper

1 small onion

3 tablespoons (45 mL) freshly squeezed lime juice

2 heaping tablespoons (35 mL) Summertime Salsa (page 277) or store-bought, plus extra for serving

2 cloves garlic, peeled

12 corn tortillas

Extra-virgin olive oil

1 head leaf lettuce, washed and dried

Additional toppings as desired: diced white onion, slivered jalapeño, cilantro, cotija cheese, sliced avocado, chopped tomatoes

1. Trim the excess fat off the pork and cut the meat into pieces roughly 2 inches (5 cm) in size. Don't worry if they are not even. Place the pork in a slow cooker. Sprinkle with cumin, salt and pepper. Slice the onion and break it apart over the pork. Add the lime juice, Summertime Salsa and garlic.

2. Add enough water to barely cover the pork. Cover with the lid and cook on high for 4 hours or on low for about 7 hours. The pork should be tender and fall apart easily. Shred the pork with a fork, toss in a bowl with a few tablespoons of the juices and keep warm.

3. When ready to assemble, brush the tortillas lightly with olive oil and fry them in a skillet to warm them; ideally you want them soft and flexible, with no real colouring. As they're cooked, wrap them in a clean tea towel to keep them warm and soft.

4. To enjoy, line tortillas with lettuce leaves (this prevents soggy tortillas) and pile on the shredded pork and desired toppings. Serve with Summertime Salsa and sour cream.

Mild Chicken and Chickpea Curry

A well-stocked pantry is the backbone of this comforting classic, using onions, spices and cans of tomatoes, chickpeas and coconut milk. In winter I bulk up this curry with cubes of sweet potato. In summer I round it out with slices of baby zucchini. And in fall, 3 cups (750 mL) chopped fresh tomatoes replace the canned ones. It's a versatile dish; I've probably made fifty variations, and we love it every way. Served over Basic Brown Rice Pilaf (page 235) or whole wheat couscous, this simple curry is a mainstay at our family table. My Strawberry Rhubarb Chutney (page 273) also makes an excellent condiment.

Since it is freezer-friendly and even better on the second day, I often make a double batch.

2 tablespoons (30 mL) Golden Ghee (page 223) or coconut oil

3 medium onions, chopped

2 cloves garlic, minced

1 inch (2.5 cm) fresh ginger, peeled and grated

2 teaspoons (10 mL) garam masala

2 teaspoons (10 mL) curry powder

1 cinnamon stick

2½ pounds (1.125 kg) boneless, skinless chicken thighs

1 can (28 ounces/796 mL) diced tomatoes

1 can (14 ounces/400 mL) full-fat coconut milk

1 cup (250 mL) chicken stock

1 teaspoon (5 mL) fine sea salt

1 can (14 ounces/398 mL) chickpeas, rinsed and drained

Full-fat plain organic yogurt, for garnish (optional)

Cilantro, for garnish

1. Melt the Golden Ghee in a large pot over medium-low heat. Tumble in the chopped onions and cook for 8 minutes, or until soft, stirring occasionally. Add the garlic, ginger, garam masala, curry powder and cinnamon stick. Cook for 2 minutes, scraping the bottom of the pot and stirring to toast the spices.

2. Push the onions to the side of the pot and add the chicken thighs. Cook for 5 minutes, turning them halfway.

3. Pour in the tomatoes, coconut milk and stock. Stir everything gently. Add the salt and chickpeas. Bring to a simmer over medium heat and cook slowly for 1 hour, uncovered. Alternatively, transfer everything to a slow cooker and cook on low for 4 to 5 hours.

4. Taste and adjust the seasoning if necessary. Serve over whole wheat couscous or Basic Brown Rice Pilaf with a dab of yogurt and torn fresh cilantro.

Quick Crustless Ham and Cheese Quiche

SERVES 4

In a perfect world, my quiches would be a deliberate and well-balanced pairing of gourmet ingredients such as bacon, wild mushrooms, broccoli rabe and crème fraîche baked inside a buttery crust. But in reality, quiche is always a last-minute dinner in our house, cobbled together with odds and ends from the refrigerator when there is absolutely nothing left to cook. We always have eggs, thanks to our chickens, as well as the ends of cheese and carrots, which are a regular vegetable in my kitchen, whatever the season.

I also don't make a crust, because if I had to roll pastry while tired and hungry, I'd *never* make quiche for dinner. So this is our not so glamorous but ever so scrumptious crustless quiche, and it can be adapted to accept your leftovers, too. Most any cooked meat, firm cheese and cooked vegetables will do just fine.

Let the kids help put this quiche together by grating cheese, beating eggs and peeling the carrot. Serve with Basic Brown Rice Pilaf (page 235) or a green salad. I also like to top mine with a generous spoonful of Summertime Salsa (page 277) or Any-Season Salsa (page 248).

2 tablespoons (30 mL) salted butter, softened	½ teaspoon (2 mL) freshly ground black pepper	2 green onions, sliced
¼ cup (60 mL) panko crumbs	1 cup (250 mL) whole milk	2 tablespoons (30 mL) chopped fresh parsley
8 large eggs	1 cup (250 mL) grated cheddar, Emmental or Gruyère cheese, divided	4 to 5 slices ham, shredded
½ teaspoon (2 mL) fine sea salt		1 large carrot, peeled into thin strips

1. Preheat oven to 400°F (200°C).

2. Generously butter the bottom and sides of a 2-quart (2 L) gratin dish. Sprinkle with panko to coat the bottom. Working over your sink to catch the crumbs, tilt the pan so that the panko goes all the way up the sides.

3. Crack the eggs into a medium bowl. Add the salt and pepper and whisk until foamy. Pour in the milk and whisk again. Reserve 1 cup (250 mL) of this mixture and pour the rest into the prepared pan.

4. Sprinkle ½ cup (125 mL) of the cheese, the green onions and the parsley over the egg mixture. Arrange the shredded ham and carrot strips evenly over the egg mixture. Top with the reserved egg mixture and the remaining ½ cup (125 mL) cheese.

5. Bake for 30 to 35 minutes, until the centre is set when you shake the pan and the sides are golden brown. Serve at once.

Roast Beef with Yorkshire Pudding

SERVES 6 · REQUIRES TIME FOR PREP

I could write an entire chapter on the subject of Sunday roasts, and in fact I did in my first cookbook, *Brown Eggs and Jam Jars*. I suppose our loyalty to the classic duo of roast beef and Yorkshire pudding stems from my British background, as it is a highly regarded meal around our family table. My children consider Yorkshire puddings to be the food of the gods and prefer a tender slice of roast beef over a steak any day.

Cooking a roast isn't that daunting once you've done it once. Equip yourself with a good probe meat thermometer and you're all set. This recipe serves at least 6, with leftover roast beef to pair with Green Olive Tapenade (page 76) for a few sandwiches during the week.

Yorkshire puddings

3 large eggs, at room temperature

½ teaspoon (2 mL) fine sea salt

1 cup (250 mL) milk, at room temperature

Scant 1 cup (250 mL) all-purpose flour

2 to 3 tablespoons (30 to 45 mL) extra-virgin olive oil

Roast beef

2 cloves garlic, minced

1 tablespoon (15 mL) grainy mustard

½ teaspoon (2 mL) dried rosemary or thyme, crumbled

½ teaspoon (2 mL) fine sea salt

½ teaspoon (2 mL) freshly ground black pepper

2 tablespoons (30 mL) extra-virgin olive oil

1 boneless top sirloin roast (4 pounds/1.8 kg)

¼ cup (60 mL) dry red wine

2 tablespoons (30 mL) unsalted butter, cubed

1. **PREPARE THE YORKSHIRE PUDDINGS** In a medium bowl, beat the eggs and the salt with a whisk until frothy. Pour in the milk and whisk again. Add the flour and whisk until there are no lumps and small bubbles appear on the surface of the batter. Cover the batter with plastic wrap and refrigerate for at least 1 hour or overnight.

2. Preheat oven to 450°F (230°C). Oil a heavy roasting pan.

3. **ROAST THE BEEF** In a small bowl, stir together the garlic, mustard, rosemary, salt, pepper and olive oil. Rub mixture all over the beef and place it in the roasting pan. Roast for 15 minutes. Reduce the oven temperature to 350°F (180°C) and roast for an additional 1 hour, or until a meat thermometer inserted into the thickest part reads 130°F (55°C) for medium-rare. Let rest, tented loosely with foil, while you bake the Yorkshire puddings.

4. **BAKE THE YORKSHIRE PUDDINGS** Immediately increase the oven temperature to 425°F (220°C) and generously oil a 12-cup muffin tin. When oven is hot, heat muffin tin in the oven for 1 minute. Beat Yorkshire pudding batter until

small bubbles rise to the surface. Remove pan from oven and quickly distribute the batter evenly among the 12 cups. Return to oven as speedily as possible and bake for 18 to 20 minutes, or until golden brown. Do NOT open the oven for any reason or the puddings will fall.

5.   Meanwhile, make the red wine sauce. Transfer the roast to a carving board and keep it tented with foil so that it stays warm. Place the roasting pan on the stove over medium heat and scrape all the drippings off the bottom. Pour in red wine and bring to a simmer. Whisk in cold butter, bit by bit, until the sauce is creamy. Season with salt and pepper, then strain the sauce through a fine-mesh sieve into a gravy boat. Keep warm.

6.   Pop Yorkshire Puddings into a waiting napkin-lined basket. Serve immediately, alongside carved roast beef, red wine sauce and roasted vegetables of your choosing.

Braised Lamb with Olives and Tomatoes

SERVES 4 TO 6

The recipe comes from my sister-in-law Laura, who also keeps it in regular rotation for her brood, no matter the season. The patio doors in Laura's dining room lead out to a rock garden boasting many varieties of thyme, and she's admitted to occasionally digging through snow in an apron and boots to find thyme for this dish. The recipe is well worth any trouble you may go through to source the ingredients because the method to bring them together is so simple.

We scoop our braised lamb over little mountains of Basic Brown Rice Pilaf (page 235), but it would be delicious over hilly mashed potatoes as well.

1 tablespoon (15 mL) extra-virgin olive oil

1 boneless lamb shoulder roast (4½ pounds/2 kg), cut into 2-inch (5 cm) chunks

¼ teaspoon (1 mL) salt

¼ teaspoon (1 mL) freshly ground pepper

2 onions, cut into ½-inch (1 cm) slices

1 tablespoon (15 mL) minced garlic

1 teaspoon (5 mL) fresh thyme leaves, plus extra for garnish

¼ cup (60 mL) dry red wine

¼ cup (60 mL) Basic Vegetable Stock (page 231)

2 medium tomatoes, chopped

¾ cup (175 mL) Kalamata olives, pitted and rinsed

1. Preheat oven to 350°F (180°C).

2. Heat the olive oil in a French oven over medium-high heat. Working in batches, season lamb with salt and pepper and carefully add to hot oil. Brown for 2 minutes on each side, turning the lamb with tongs.

3. Remove lamb and set aside. Add the onions to the same pot and cook until soft, about 5 minutes. Add garlic and thyme; cook for an additional minute. Scrape the onions to the side and deglaze the pot with the red wine, scraping up any bits from the bottom of the pot. Stir in the Basic Vegetable Stock and tomatoes. Return the lamb to the pot, along with any accumulated juices.

4. Bring everything to a simmer and then cover and place in the oven. Braise for 1 hour. Turn the meat, add the olives and return to the oven for 45 minutes to 1 hour, until the lamb is falling apart.

5. Lightly shred the meat and season with a touch of black pepper. Serve garnished with fresh thyme leaves.

TIP: *This recipe may be made with 4 lamb shanks instead of shoulder. It can also be prepared with a leg of lamb (I've done it all!): simply double all the other ingredients and increase the cooking time by about half an hour.*

Whole Simmered Chicken

MAKES 5 CUPS (1.25 L) COOKED CHICKEN, 10 CUPS (2.5 L) CHICKEN STOCK

A boiled chicken is one of the best ways get a jump-start on a week's worth of meals. Everything comes together in a few minutes, using traditional aromatics or whatever you have on hand. The chicken is simmered slowly and then cooled in the broth, which makes for very tender, flavourful meat and a clear, fragrant stock.

One bird yields enough shredded chicken and stock for a main dish and a soup for our family of five. I use the meat in my Tangy Quinoa Carrot Chicken Salad (page 75), lunch box wraps, Every-Season Risotto (page 189) or a frequent request of my children, chicken and cheese quesadillas. Of course you can use it as a springboard for chicken pot pie or chicken noodle soup.

If you can, use a grain-fed, organic chicken, as they tend to be much leaner than typical commercial birds. Or just skim off the excess fat from the surface as the chicken simmers.

1 whole organic chicken (about 5 pounds/2.25 kg)	3 small carrots, peeled and roughly chopped	½ teaspoon (2 mL) black peppercorns
1 medium leek or onion, roughly chopped	3 stalks celery, roughly chopped	4 or 5 sprigs fresh thyme or parsley
	1 bay leaf	1 teaspoon (5 mL) fine sea salt

1. Place the chicken breast side down in a stock pot. Add the leek, carrots, celery, bay leaf and peppercorns. Cover the chicken and vegetables with room-temperature water.

2. Partially cover the pot with a lid and bring to a rapid boil over high heat. Boil for 1 minute, then reduce heat to low. Skim off any foam. Add the thyme and salt.

3. Simmer the chicken, partially covered, for 45 minutes. Using a sturdy pair of tongs, flip the chicken so it's breast side up. Simmer for another 45 minutes. Turn off heat and let the chicken cool in the broth until lukewarm.

4. Scoop out the chicken and shred the meat off the bones. Strain the broth into jars and discard the carcass and vegetables. Store the shredded chicken in an airtight container in the refrigerator for up to 3 days, or cover with broth and freeze for up to 6 months. Store broth in the freezer for up to 1 year.

TIP: *Add a slice or two of fresh ginger and a few cloves of garlic to turn the broth into a flu-fighting magic elixir.*

Butternut Squash Casserole with Apple and Leek

SERVES 4 TO 6

⁂

You know that Thanksgiving side dish that always upstages the turkey? This casserole is one such culprit. It's a celebration of fall and winter produce, featuring butternut squash, sweet apples and tender leek. With a dash of nutmeg, it's irresistible comfort food and should definitely not be reserved only for holidays. It can be prepared ahead of time and baked an hour before dinner.

2 pounds (900 g) butternut squash

2 teaspoons (10 mL) extra-virgin olive oil

1 large leek, white and pale green parts only

2 tablespoons (30 mL) Golden Ghee (page 223) or unsalted butter

1 green apple

1 large egg

1 cup (250 mL) freshly grated Parmesan cheese, divided

½ cup (125 mL) panko crumbs, divided

3 tablespoons (45 mL) mayonnaise

½ teaspoon (2 mL) sea salt

½ teaspoon (2 mL) freshly ground black pepper

¼ teaspoon (1 mL) freshly grated nutmeg

1. Peel and seed the squash, then cut it into ½-inch (1 cm) cubes, yielding about 4 heaping cups (1.125 L). Place in a large pot, cover with water and bring to a boil over high heat. Boil squash for 10 minutes, or until fork-tender but still able to hold its shape. Drain well and cool.

2. Preheat oven to 350°F (180°C). Grease a 3-quart (3 L) baking dish with the olive oil.

3. Quarter the leek lengthwise and cut into ½-inch (1 cm) pieces.

4. In a large saucepan, melt the Golden Ghee over medium heat. Add the leeks and stir to coat them in the ghee. Partially cover and cook gently, stirring occasionally, until very soft but not browning, 8 to 10 minutes.

5. Meanwhile, core the apple and cut it into ½-inch (1 cm) cubes. Add the apple to the leeks and cook for 2 minutes. Remove from heat and cool.

6. In a large bowl, beat together the egg, ¾ cup (175 mL) of the Parmesan, ¼ cup (60 mL) of the panko, the mayonnaise, salt, pepper and nutmeg. Gently but thoroughly fold in the cooked squash and the leek and apple mixture. Scrape the squash mixture into the prepared baking dish.

7. Stir together the remaining ¼ cup (60 mL) Parmesan and ¼ cup (60 mL) panko. Sprinkle over the casserole. Bake for 45 to 50 minutes, until the top is light golden. Serve hot.

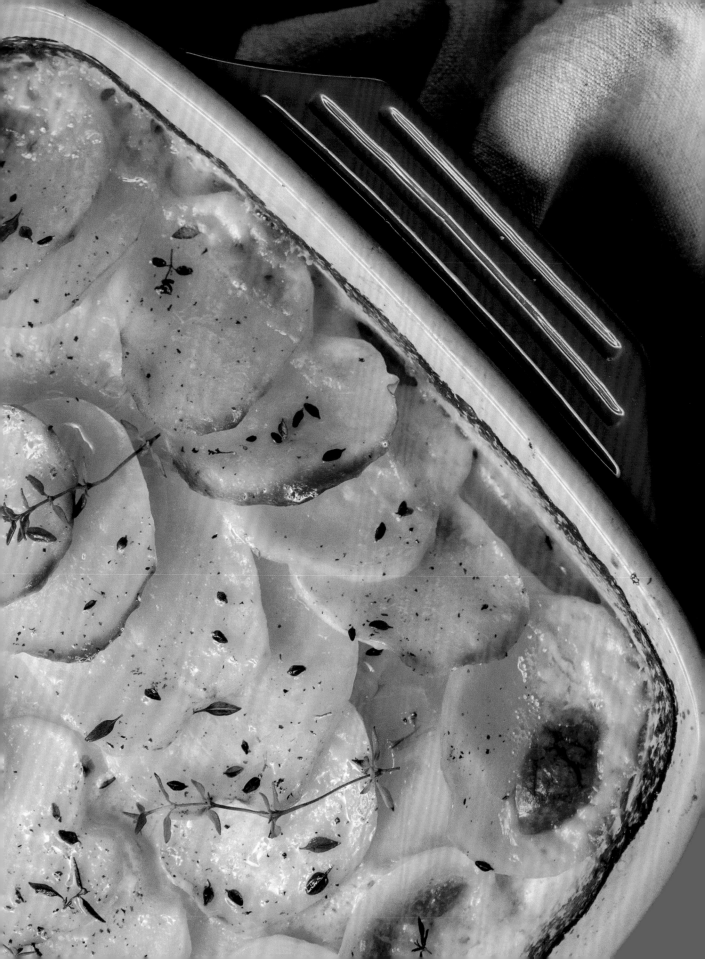

Roasted Garlic Scalloped Potatoes

SERVES 6

Put aside any recollections of bland, watery scalloped potatoes from the Easter dinners of your youth and open your mind to thyme-scented layers of velvety potatoes, wrapped in a cream infused with roasted garlic. If the crispy-edged slices on the top don't convince you that these are the best scalloped potatoes ever, then the ultra-creamy layers underneath definitely will.

Scalloped potatoes are a lovely accompaniment to a Sunday roast beef or a Quick Crustless Ham and Cheese Quiche (page 206). They reheat beautifully, thanks to all the cream keeping them moist, and are one of my favourite side dishes to serve when entertaining for dinner.

1 head of garlic

2 teaspoons (10 mL) extra-virgin olive oil, divided

2½ pounds (1.125 kg) yellow-fleshed potatoes

1½ cups (375 mL) heavy (35%) cream

1 teaspoon (5 mL) fine sea salt

¾ teaspoon (4 mL) freshly ground black pepper

3 teaspoons (15 mL) fresh thyme leaves, divided

1. Preheat oven to 375°F (190°C).

2. Slice ¼ inch (5 mm) off the top of the head of garlic to expose the tops of the cloves. Place on a 10-inch (25 cm) square of foil. Drizzle 1 teaspoon (5 mL) of the olive oil over the garlic cloves, letting the oil sink down between the cloves. Seal tightly in the foil. Place on a pie plate and roast until tender, 40 to 50 minutes.

3. Meanwhile, peel the potatoes and rinse under cool water. Slice potatoes ⅛ inch (3 mm) thick using a mandoline or a food processor fitted with the slicer disc.

4. In a small saucepan, heat the cream over medium-low heat until warm. Sprinkle in the salt and pepper and stir to dissolve the salt. Carefully unwrap the roasted garlic (it will be very hot) and cool slightly. Turn the head upside down and squeeze out the soft cloves into the cream. Discard the papery garlic skins. Mash the garlic into the cream with the back of a fork.

5. Grease a 9-inch (2.5 L) square baking dish with the remaining 1 teaspoon (5 mL) olive oil. Arrange a layer of potatoes over the bottom of the pan (about one-third of the potatoes). Pour ½ cup (125 mL) of the garlic cream over them. Scatter with 1 teaspoon (5 mL) of the fresh thyme leaves. Repeat to make two more layers, ending with the remaining thyme leaves.

6. Bake for 55 to 60 minutes, until potatoes are tender when pierced with a fork and the top is lightly browned. Cool slightly to set the dish, then serve hot.

Simple Bites Staples

I've been making my own vinaigrettes and pesto since I was about eight years old, and now I've got my kids hooked on those familiar flavours, too. Why? Personal taste and satisfaction. They trigger happy childhood memories like no bottled product would and they taste far superior to anything money can buy. For me, that rewarding feeling of making my own staples can't be replaced with the promise of convenience. There's more to it, of course. Pantry staples prepared from scratch are far more nourishing to your diet than their processed counterparts. They are unbeatably fresh and endlessly customizable, once you get the hang of the recipes and methods. Add on the elimination of packaging and the money to be saved and you have a solid case for homemade kitchen staples.

This chapter includes staples that I could not do without. There's creamy Coconut Almond Milk (page 227) that lets me enjoy a bowl of granola or muesli again after realizing that milk no longer agrees with me. Basil and Pepita Pesto (page 247) shows up in a few varieties, because it's the best way to use up excess homegrown herbs in the fall. My Basic Vegetable Stock (page 231) rescues withering produce and turns them into broth for our beloved Every-Season Risotto (page 189). You may not think my homemade Lighter Ricotta (page 224) will change your life, but try it on Pepper Parmesan Crackers (page 98) with Gin-Cured Gravlax (page 151) or atop Roasted Cauliflower with Quick Tomato Sauce (page 127) and you may be convinced. And where would we be without our Everyday Vinaigrette (page 232), the oil-and-vinegar dressing that got all three of my kids hooked on green salads?

These foods are the backbone of my kitchen, along with a lineup of canned goods from the "Preserves Pantry" chapter. You can find my stamp on them, as with most homemade foods, but I encourage you to make the recipes your own. Perhaps you like your everyday salad dressing to have more of a garlic punch or feature another kind of vinegar. Heat up Any-Season Salsa (page 248) with a few extra jalapeños or toss your favourite dried fruit and nuts into my Fig, Rosemary and Pistachio Crisps (page 239).

Be a brave cook and baker, willing to experiment to learn what works for you. Start small, with a simple stock or salad dressing, incorporating these staples into your usual workflow without getting overwhelmed. Then when you have a bit more time and wish to expand your kitchen knowledge, make a batch of ricotta or pie pastry. And after experimenting, if you find that buying your buttermilk, pesto and salsa still works best for you, that's okay, too. No one, no matter how knowledgeable, can decide what's best for you to make in your kitchen. I certainly wouldn't dream of it. This chapter of staples merely suggests what you might want to make instead of buying for taste, health, financial and eco-friendly benefits. I'm convinced, however, that once you try a few recipes, you'll be inspired to keep going.

Golden Ghee

MAKES ⅔ TO 1 CUP (150 TO 250 ML)

A few ingredients have a permanent place on my kitchen counter: good-quality sea salt, extra-virgin olive oil, fresh black pepper—and a jar of ghee. This clarified butter derivative is shelf stable and doesn't go rancid at room temperature the way butter will. I reach for it in the morning for my eggs or Egg-Topped Umami Oatmeal (page 47) and in the evening for dinners like Mild Chicken and Chickpea Curry (page 205) and Basic Brown Rice Pilaf (page 235). Once you see how simple ghee is to make, you'll seldom go without.

If you can find it, organic, grass-fed butter is best. And don't worry if your homemade ghee is grainy—it's a sign that you're doing it right.

1 pound (450 g) organic unsalted butter

1. Place a fine-mesh sieve over a bowl or large measuring cup and line it with several layers of cheesecloth.

2. Cut butter into 1-inch (2.5 cm) cubes. Place in a medium, heavy pot over medium heat and stir it occasionally as it melts. When the butter begins to simmer and a white foam forms on the top, reduce the heat to medium-low. Set a timer for about 20 minutes and follow the visual cues below.

3. After about 5 minutes, the foam will subside and bubbles will appear. Then, as the butter continues to cook, it will become more translucent as the milk solids sink to the bottom. The bubbles will be slightly larger. Stir occasionally.

4. After about 15 minutes, the butter will start to look more golden and the bubbles will be much bigger, about 1 to 2 inches (5 cm) in diameter. Stir it frequently so the solids don't burn. Watch for the butter to foam white for a second time, although the foam will be slightly less thick than the first time. This is the visual indicator that the ghee is ready. Remove the pot from the heat and let it cool for a minute.

5. Carefully pour the ghee over the cheesecloth, leaving behind the brown milk solids in the pot. Transfer the hot ghee to a clean 1-pint (500 mL) jar. Cover loosely with a clean towel and let sit at room temperature until solidified. Store on the counter, covered, for up to 1 month, or in the refrigerator for about 6 months.

TIP: *You can use the milk solids on popcorn, in curries or as a flavouring for soup.*

Lighter Ricotta

MAKES 1¼ CUPS (300 ML)

❧

We always ate my mother's soft goat milk cheese when we were growing up, which is probably why I still prefer my homemade ricotta on the lighter side, rather than overly rich. Nowadays I use organic cow's milk and some light cream for a soft, supple cheese that we use year round.

Watching the curds separate from the whey never gets old; neither does having homemade ricotta around for topping an Asparagus Cheddar Frittata (page 30) or Roasted Cauliflower with Quick Tomato Sauce (page 127). We spread ricotta on bagels and top that with Gin-Cured Gravlax (page 151) for an utterly unbeatable lunch.

Don't toss the whey from the cheese; use it for Spinach Crêpes with Blueberry Compote (page 32), smoothies or my Honey Whole Wheat Bagels (page 39). It will keep for a few weeks in the refrigerator.

4 cups (1 L) organic 2% milk

1 cup (250 mL) 24-hour Buttermilk (page 229) or cultured buttermilk

1 cup (250 mL) half-and-half (10%) cream

¾ teaspoon (4 mL) fine sea salt

1. Place a fine-mesh sieve over a large bowl and line it with several layers of cheesecloth or a clean tea towel.

2. If you have a thermometer, attach it to the side of a medium, heavy pot. Make sure the bottom of the thermometer is not touching the bottom of the pot or you won't get an accurate reading. Add the milk, 24-hour Buttermilk, cream and salt to the pot. Place over medium-low heat and slowly bring to a simmer, stirring occasionally. This will take 10 to 15 minutes.

3. As the mixture heats, it will become grainy, and then, somewhere between 195 and 205°F (90 and 96°C), the liquid will separate and small curds will begin to form. When you see cottage cheese–looking curds surrounded by cloudy yellow whey, remove the pot from the heat and let stand for 5 minutes.

4. Gently ladle the curds into the cheesecloth. Once most of the curds are in the cloth, tip what remains in the pot into the cheesecloth. Allow the ricotta to drain for 2 minutes for a spreadable cheese. Let the curds drain longer if you want a firmer cheese. Enjoy the ricotta warm or transfer to a jar, cover and refrigerate for up to 4 days. The whey may be frozen for up to 6 months.

Coconut Almond Milk

MAKES 3½ CUPS (875 ML) · REQUIRES TIME FOR PREP

Over the past few years, I've noticed that uncooked cow's milk disagrees with me, and this nut milk has been my replacement. I use it on my hot cereal for breakfast, in smoothies for a snack and in chia puddings for dessert. Rich and creamy, sweet and nutty—you'll never want to be without a jar on hand. I like mine with a few drops of vanilla, but if you prefer your milk to be slightly sweet, add two pitted Medjool dates to the blender with the hot water.

The milk does not reconstitute well from frozen, but it keeps beautifully in the refrigerator for up to a week.

1 cup (250 mL) raw whole almonds

1¼ cups (300 mL) unsweetened shredded coconut

½ teaspoon (2 mL) pure vanilla extract (optional)

1. In a bowl, submerge almonds in room-temperature water and soak overnight. Drain and rinse well.

2. Boil a kettle with at least 4 cups (1 L) of water. Combine soaked almonds and shredded coconut in a blender. Carefully pour in 4 cups (1 L) of very hot water. Let soak for 30 minutes.

3. Blend the mixture until very smooth and homogenous. Set a colander over a deep bowl and line it with cheesecloth. Pour in the blended mixture. Once most of the milk has drained into the bowl, gather up the corners of the cheesecloth and hang to drip for at least an hour. This will help extract the last of the milk. You can also gently squeeze the bag to get the last few drops of milk.

4. Pour the milk into a clean 1-quart (1 L) jar. If you like, keep the coconut-almond pulp to add to smoothies, oatmeal or baked goods.

5. Stir vanilla, if using, into the coconut almond milk. Cover the jar with a lid and shake well. Store in the refrigerator for up to 1 week. Shake well before using.

Homemade Buttermilk

True buttermilk is a by-product of churning cream for butter, and it is usually available only from artisan farmers. What we buy in the grocery store is cultured skim milk labelled as buttermilk and hardly worth the price tag when it is so easy to make yourself at home.

If you mainly use buttermilk for baking, as I do, any of these variations will do just fine. I've included three versions, depending on how much time you have. My favourite is the 24-hour Buttermilk, which I use for my Baked Buttermilk Chicken Strips (page 81), Spelt Date Scones (page 35), Fig, Rosemary and Pistachio Crisps (page 239) and more.

In specialty grocery and natural food stores, you can also find buttermilk powder, which is good to have for long-term storage.

Instant Buttermilk

MAKES 1 CUP (250 ML)

½ cup (125 mL) full-fat plain organic yogurt

½ cup (125 mL) 2% milk

1. Whisk together the yogurt and milk. Use as directed in the recipe. If necessary, store in the refrigerator for up to 3 days.

10-minute Buttermilk

MAKES 1 CUP (250 ML)

1 cup (250 mL) 2% milk

1 tablespoon (15 mL) white vinegar or freshly squeezed lemon juice

1. Whisk together the milk and vinegar. Let stand for 10 minutes before using as directed in the recipe. If necessary, store in the refrigerator for up to 3 days.

24-hour Buttermilk

MAKES 2 CUPS (500 ML) · REQUIRES TIME FOR PREP

2 cups (500 mL) whole milk

2 tablespoons (30 mL) cultured buttermilk or sour cream

1. Fill a 1-quart (1 L) jar with hot water to warm it and get a jump-start on the process. Pour out the water.

2. Combine the milk and cultured buttermilk in the jar and stir to combine. Cover the jar with a lid and place in a warm spot in your kitchen. Label the jar with the date and time. When the buttermilk is ready, it will have thickened slightly and have a tangy taste. This will take anywhere from 12 to 24 hours, depending on how warm your kitchen is.

3. Store buttermilk in the refrigerator and use within 2 weeks. Shake before using.

Basic Vegetable Stock

MAKES 2 QUARTS (2 L) · REQUIRES TIME FOR PREP

Making your own vegetable stock serves two main purposes: it uses up kitchen scraps that might otherwise go into the garbage or compost, and it yields a fragrant broth for other dishes.

For the scraps, use mushroom stems and trimmings, onion, leek and garlic, carrots, celery, peppers, broccoli stems, zucchini, stems of herbs and anything else you have available. For a darker, more robust stock, roast the vegetables before simmering the stock. Both methods are included here.

4 to 6 cups (1 to 1.5 L) vegetable scraps	½ teaspoon (2 mL) black peppercorns
2 to 4 cloves garlic	1 tablespoon (15 mL) tomato paste (for dark stock)
1 bay leaf	

CLEAR VEGETABLE STOCK

1. Combine vegetable scraps, garlic, bay leaf and peppercorns in a 5-quart (5 L) pot. Cover with cold water and bring to a boil over high heat. Immediately reduce heat to medium and simmer stock, uncovered, for 1 hour.

2. Cool stock to lukewarm, then strain into a bowl, discarding the vegetable scraps. Cool completely at room temperature.

3. Pour stock into clean mason jars or plastic containers and store in the refrigerator for up to 5 days or in the freezer for up to 6 months.

DARK VEGETABLE STOCK

1. Preheat oven to 450°F (230°C).

2. Toss scraps and garlic lightly with the tomato paste and spread in a shallow roasting pan. Roast for 20 to 30 minutes (depending on the size and variety of scraps) until caramelized, but not charred in any way.

3. Transfer roasted vegetables to a 5-quart (5 L) pot. Add the bay leaf and peppercorns. Cover with cold water and bring to a boil over high heat. Immediately reduce heat to medium and simmer stock, uncovered, for 1 hour

4. Cool stock to lukewarm, then strain into a bowl, discarding the vegetable scraps. Cool completely at room temperature.

5. Pour stock into clean mason jars or plastic containers and store in the refrigerator for up to 5 days or in the freezer for up to 6 months.

Everyday Vinaigrette

MAKES ½ CUP (125 ML)

❧

I've made a lot of mistakes as a mother, but when I watch my children tuck enthusiastically into a heaping plate of green salad, I feel proud that at least I did one thing right.

Their love of salad wasn't born overnight; in fact the boys preferred a bowl of plain, undressed lettuce for the longest time. One day I introduced them to greens dressed with just a squeeze of lemon and a pinch of salt. A few months later I could add a drizzle of olive oil, too. Finally, the day came when I could dress a salad with my favourite tangy vinaigrette, toss in a few vegetables or toasted seeds and serve it to the whole family. Clara emulates everything her big brothers do, right down to the salad eating, so that was never an issue. Now we enjoy a simple tossed green salad at least three evenings a week—and this recipe is our favourite all-purpose vinaigrette.

A salad dressing is only as good as its ingredients, so be sure to use only fresh lemon and freshly ground black pepper, and choose the best olive oil you can afford. This vinaigrette is delicious with all greens from all seasons.

1 small clove garlic, minced

½ teaspoon (2 mL) sea salt

2 tablespoons (30 mL) freshly squeezed lemon juice

1 tablespoon (15 mL) white wine vinegar

1 teaspoon (5 mL) Dijon mustard

¼ teaspoon (1 mL) freshly ground black pepper

6 tablespoons (90 mL) extra-virgin olive oil

1. In a small bowl using a wooden spoon, or using a mortar and pestle, pulverize the garlic with the salt to make a paste.

2. Add the lemon juice, white wine vinegar, mustard and black pepper. Stir to combine. Slowly drizzle in the olive oil, whisking until it is emulsified and creamy.

3. Transfer to a jar and cover. Vinaigrette will keep for a few days at room temperature or in the refrigerator for up to 1 week. Bring to room temperature and shake well before using.

TIP: *Ask an expert to recommend an olive oil specifically for salads. You'll appreciate the full flavour, aroma and health benefits of a high-quality olive oil that you won't be heating.*

Basic Brown Rice Pilaf

SERVES 6

If you're thinking that rice is merely a boring accompaniment to the main dish, think again. It can be the base for healthy salads full of toasted seeds and shredded vegetables or an addition to hearty soups. Rice can inspire a lunch box sushi bowl or a quick breakfast fix topped with green onions and a fried egg. My family's favourite rice is brown basmati, and this pilaf is our preferred cooking method.

The slow, constant heat of the oven does wonders for brown rice, which has a tendency to be either mushy or crunchy when cooked on the stovetop. Baked in the oven, each grain is perfectly fluffed and the nutty flavour shines through. A little sautéed onion and a bay leaf help to turn what could be an ordinary side dish into a comforting and fragrant pilaf.

2 cups (500 mL) long-grain brown basmati rice

1 tablespoon (15 mL) Golden Ghee (page 223) or unsalted butter

1 teaspoon (5 mL) extra-virgin olive oil

½ medium onion, diced

1 bay leaf

1 teaspoon (5 mL) sea salt

3½ cups (875 mL) water

1. Preheat oven to 375°F (190°C).

2. Rinse rice in a fine-mesh sieve and drain well. In a French oven, melt the Golden Ghee and olive oil together over medium heat. Add the onion and bay leaf and cook for 2 minutes. Add rice and salt, stir well to combine and toast for 2 minutes, stirring occasionally.

3. Add the water and bring to a boil. Stir the rice once, then cover and transfer to the oven. Bake for 40 minutes. Remove from oven and let sit, covered, for an additional 10 minutes.

4. Fluff rice with a fork and serve hot with your favourite main dish.

SIMPLE BITES STAPLES

235

HOW TO COOK PULSES

Chances are you already cook with beans, chickpeas, lentils and dried peas but didn't know that they are all pulses, and one of Canada's largest crops. Pulses are drought tolerant and require very little water to grow. Including pulses in your regular meal planning means eating local, eating for health and eating one of the most cost-effective proteins around.

Dry and canned pulses are key staples in our pantry. I consider them essential for snacks such as hummus or roasted chickpeas, handy for rounding out soups and salads, and unbeatable for meatless main dishes. Most of the time, I choose to cook beans, chickpeas and lentils from dry because the taste is far superior to anything that comes in a can. It's also more affordable to cook pulses from dry, and you can control the amount of salt you add.

Here is a list of dried pulses and how to prepare them. As a general rule, 1 cup (250 mL) dried beans will yield 3 cups (750 mL) cooked.

BEANS

adzuki, black, black-eyed peas, kidney, Great Northern, navy, pinto, fava, small red, mung, lima, cranberry, pink and dozens of heirloom varieties

CHICKPEAS

Also known as garbanzo beans; Kabuli (larger) and Desi (smaller)

PEAS

split green and yellow, whole green and yellow

LENTILS

green, red, small brown, French green/du Puy and black/beluga

DRIED BEANS, CHICKPEAS AND PEAS (REQUIRES TIME FOR PREP)

1. Begin by picking over the dried pulses and discarding any small pebbles. Rinse well under running water.

2. Soak for 8 to 12 hours before cooking. This is not absolutely necessary, but it does cut down on the cooking time, and some say it reduces the, *ahem*, side effects of eating pulses.

3. Drain pulses, place in a saucepan and add water to cover by a few inches. Do not salt pulses during the cooking, as salt can cause them to toughen and in some cases, never even become tender. Season *after* they are cooked, but while they are still warm, so the pulses can absorb the salt.

4. Bring to a boil over high heat. Skim off any scum that comes to the surface, and lower the heat to a simmer. Continue to cook, uncovered, until the pulses are tender, stirring occasionally and adding more water when needed to keep them covered. Always keep them at a simmer; boiling can cause the cooking liquid to evaporate too quickly, as well as cause the pulses to break apart.

5. Cooking times will vary with quality, amount and freshness of the pulses; it can take from 1 to 2 hours. Check them regularly after the first hour. Pulses are cooked when they can be easily mashed between two fingers or with a fork.

6. Once cooked, season with salt while still warm. Store in their cooking liquid in the refrigerator for up to 1 week. They also freeze very well, so be sure to stash some away for a quick meal on another day.

DRIED LENTILS

1. Begin by picking over the lentils and discarding any small pebbles. Rinse well under running water. After they're rinsed, lentils can be cooked right away. Use 2 cups (500 mL) of water for each 1 cup (250 mL) of lentils. Do not add salt during the cooking. Bring them to a vigorous boil, then reduce heat to medium-low and simmer, uncovered, for about 20 minutes. Taste them along the way; depending on their freshness, they will take less or more time to cook. They will absorb the water and plump up nicely.

2. Once cooked, drain if necessary and season with salt while still warm. Store in their cooking liquid in the refrigerator for up to 1 week. They also freeze very well, so be sure to stash some away for a quick meal on another day.

Fig, Rosemary and Pistachio Crisps

MAKES 8 DOZEN

These highly addicting crisps are delicately flavoured with buttermilk and honey and scented with fresh rosemary. They contain just enough nuts and dried fruits to complement the accompaniments on a cheese board. My good friend and food writer Julie Van Rosendaal first baked up a version and inspired me to play around with the flavours. Now they are my standard cracker for entertaining, and they beat out all the other nibbles on the table every time.

The recipe can be done over two days, as you need to let the loaves cool sufficiently before slicing and crisping them.

1 cup (250 mL) whole wheat bread flour

1 cup (250 mL) all-purpose flour

2 teaspoons (10 mL) baking soda

½ teaspoon (2 mL) fine sea salt

1 cup (250 mL) chopped dried figs

½ cup (125 mL) chopped pistachios

½ cup (125 mL) raw pepitas

¼ cup (60 mL) sesame seeds

¼ cup (60 mL) ground flaxseed

1 tablespoon (15 mL) finely chopped fresh rosemary

2 cups (500 mL) Homemade Buttermilk (page 228) or store-bought

¼ cup (60 mL) Demerara sugar

¼ cup (60 mL) liquid honey, warmed

Zest of 1 orange

1. Preheat oven to 350°F (180°C). Grease 4 mini loaf pans with oil and line bottoms with parchment paper.

2. In a large bowl, stir together the whole wheat flour, all-purpose flour, baking soda and salt. Add the figs, pistachios, pepitas, sesame seeds, flaxseed and rosemary. Stir just until everything is coated in the flour.

3. In a small bowl, stir together the Homemade Buttermilk, sugar, honey and orange zest until the honey is incorporated. Add the liquid to the flour mixture and mix together until just combined.

4. Divide the batter among the loaf pans. Bake for 20 to 22 minutes, until golden and springy to the touch. Remove loaves from the pans and cool completely on a wire rack. Once cooled, wrap tightly in plastic wrap and chill or partially freeze before slicing.

(recipe continues)

5. Preheat oven to 300°F (150°C). Set the oven racks in the upper and lower third positions.

6. Remove the plastic wrap. Using a serrated knife, slice the loaves as thinly as you can (aim for ⅛ inch/3 mm thickness if possible) and place the slices in a single layer on 2 ungreased cookie sheets. Bake for 15 minutes, then turn them over and bake for another 15 to 20 minutes, until deep golden. They will crisp up as they cool.

7. Cool completely on wire racks. Store in an airtight container at room temperature for up to 1 week or freeze for up to 6 months.

TIP: *The loaves may also be baked in 2 standard loaf pans instead of the mini-pans. If using standard loaf pans, bake for about 45 minutes.*

Lemon Herb Finishing Salt

With the help of a food processor and a quick stint in the oven, you can infuse salts with herbs, flowers, citrus and more. These perfumed salts are a wonderful way to add a small burst of flavour to pastas, salads, mains and appetizers.

Try sprinkling the salt on cuts of meat, fish or roast potatoes and vegetables. Finish a salad with the lemon salt, or simply season a bowl of buttered popcorn.

2 cups (500 mL) coarse salt, such as kosher

¼ cup (60 mL) loosely packed fresh sage leaves

¼ cup (60 mL) loosely packed fresh rosemary leaves

¼ cup (60 mL) loosely packed fresh thyme leaves

4 whole lemons, scrubbed

1. Preheat oven to 250°F (120°C).

2. Make sure there are no stems on the herbs, just leaves. Combine the salt, sage, rosemary and thyme in a food processor. Process until the herbs are finely chopped.

3. Line a large rimmed baking sheet with parchment paper and pour the salt into a pile in the middle of the paper.

4. Zest the lemons directly onto the salt. This way, any of the essential oils that spray will be absorbed by the salt as well. Rub the zest into the salt with your fingertips. (Your hands are going to smell wonderful!) Spread the salt evenly around the pan.

5. Bake for about 15 minutes, until the salt feels dry and the zest looks dehydrated. Let cool completely on the baking sheet. Break apart any chunks with your fingers, or blitz again in the food processor to break up any clumps. Transfer your lemon herb finishing salt to a jar. Seal with a lid and label jar with the recipe and date. Use within a year.

Autumn Spice Blend

MAKES ½ CUP (125 ML)

❧

I reach for this five-spice blend constantly in the fall and winter months. It brings a touch of excitement to everything from Noah's French Toast with Cinnamon Maple Butter (page 42) to Whole-Grain Gingerbread Waffles with Molasses Cinnamon Syrup (page 44), granola, scones, cookies, hot cocoa and all sorts of holiday baking.

As much as possible, the spices should be freshly ground or grated. I keep a cheap electric blade grinder in my kitchen that is dedicated to spices. It grinds up the dark and mysterious allspice, which contains the same natural oils as pepper, cloves, ginger and cinnamon. Cloves are essential to this blend, but in small amounts, whereas ginger plays a strong supporting role to the cinnamon. A dusting of nutmeg adds the finishing touch, freshly grated from a whole seed.

Store the spice blend in your freezer to preserve the freshness of the flavours and use with abandon.

⅓ cup (75 mL) ground cinnamon (see Tip)

2 tablespoons (30 mL) ground ginger

1 tablespoon (15 mL) freshly grated nutmeg (1 small nutmeg seed)

2 teaspoons (10 mL) ground allspice

½ teaspoon (2 mL) ground cloves

1. In a small bowl, sift together the cinnamon, ginger, nutmeg, allspice and cloves. Stir well to combine thoroughly.

2. Transfer spice blend to a clean, dry jar and cover with an airtight lid. Label jar with the recipe and date. Use spice blend within 2 weeks or store in the freezer and use within 3 months.

TIP: *I use a blend of both Ceylon and cassia in my spice mix. It is a little known fact, but most cinnamon available in supermarkets is in fact cassia, a distant cousin to true cinnamon. The best true Ceylon cinnamon comes from one place: Sri Lanka. Its papery sticks are lighter in colour and more fragile than cassia. The false cinnamon, cassia, comes from China, Vietnam and Indonesia, and its thicker, tougher sticks are a much darker brown.*

Both spices have their characteristic qualities. Cinnamon is much more complex and subtle, whereas cassia is more versatile and holds its flavour longer. I suggest cooking and baking with both to find the flavour balance you prefer.

Basil and Pepita Pesto

MAKES ⅔ CUP (150 ML)

If there is one fall tradition I uphold above all, it is making and freezing pesto. We simply must have the freezer stocked with multiple batches of homemade pesto as we head into winter. I harvest my garden herbs around the end of September; nearly all the basil is set aside for pesto—and a good bunch of the parsley and oregano, too, because we like variety in our pesto.

Traditionally, pesto is made with pine nuts, but since my boys frequently take pesto to their nut-free school in lunches such as Roasted Sweet Potato, Pesto and Bacon Wrap (page 78) and leftover pasta dishes, I make mine with pepitas instead. Pepitas are shelled pumpkin seeds, a delicious and healthy substitute to pine nuts and a lot less expensive.

2 cups (500 mL) packed fresh basil leaves	¼ cup (60 mL), raw or lightly toasted pepitas	¼ cup (60 mL) extra-virgin olive oil
1 large clove garlic, peeled	½ cup (125 mL) freshly grated Parmigiano-Reggiano	Pinch each of sea salt and freshly cracked black pepper

1. Combine basil leaves, garlic and pepitas in a food processor and finely chop for 10 to 15 seconds. Scrape down the sides of the bowl.

2. Sprinkle in the cheese and pour in the olive oil. Process until pesto is smooth, about 30 seconds. Season lightly with salt and pepper.

3. Transfer pesto to a small jar. Drizzle a little extra olive oil on the top to seal it and preserve the freshness. Store in the refrigerator for up to 2 weeks or freeze for up to 1 year.

PARSLEY PEPITA PESTO

Swap out the basil for fresh flat-leaf parsley and brighten it up with a squeeze of lemon juice. This vivid green pesto is scrumptious with roast meats, grilled fish or sliced tomato sandwiches.

OREGANO HAZELNUT PESTO

This spin on pesto uses a garden perennial that grows in abundance. Replace half the basil with fresh oregano and replace the pepitas with toasted hazelnuts. Delicious on roast chicken, lamb or squash, and a good pairing for light pasta dishes.

TIP: *Freeze in ice cube trays or muffin tins, and transfer to baggies or jars when frozen. May also be frozen in small resealable bags.*

Any-Season Salsa

Everyone needs a simple salsa that tastes fresh—even in the dead of winter. When fresh tomatoes and sweet peppers are not available, this is our everyday salsa, inspired by my sister Haidi's recipe. When we're together, she always makes an enormous batch, and yet it is never enough. We heap it on eggs, tacos—even oysters on the half shell—but most of it is consumed, one chip at a time, at the daily happy hour.

We both insist the salsa has to be handmade and does not taste the same when made in a blender. Feel free to ramp up the heat by adding an additional jalapeño.

1 can (28 ounces/796 mL) whole tomatoes or 1 quart (1 L) Canned Whole Tomatoes (page 274), drained

¼ medium sweet white onion, such as Vidalia, peeled

1 jalapeño pepper

2 cloves garlic, peeled

About ¼ bunch cilantro

½ teaspoon (2 mL) fine sea salt

Juice of ½ lime

1. Get started by placing a box grater in a medium bowl. Grate the tomatoes on the large holes, discarding the cores. Grate the onion on the large holes as well.

2. On the smaller holes of the grater, grate the bottom half of the jalapeño. Pick out the seeds and discard them. Taste a little bit of the jalapeño to gauge how hot it is. You may want to stop at half or keep going, depending on how spicy you like your salsa.

3. Grate the garlic on the smaller holes as well. Mince the cilantro and add to the bowl. Sprinkle in the salt and pour the lime juice over the mixture. Stir the salsa very well to combine.

4. Sample a spoonful of salsa, carefully considering heat, saltiness and acidity. You may want to add more jalapeño, a touch of salt or a few more drops of lime. Once you are happy with the salsa, scoop it into a bowl and serve with your favourite tortilla chips. Salsa will keep for up to 5 days in the refrigerator.

Flaky Pie Pastry

MAKES 1 (9-INCH/23 CM) DOUBLE CRUST

Pie crust was one of the first basic recipes I learned in the kitchen as a child. I remember rubbing the butter into the flour and, later, experimenting with decorative edging on my pies. I still enjoy getting my hands floury for the sake of a flaky pie crust, and this all-butter recipe is my go-to for pies of all seasons.

2¾ cups (675 mL) all-purpose flour

2 teaspoons (10 mL) raw cane sugar

½ teaspoon (2 mL) fine sea salt

1 cup (250 mL) cold unsalted butter

½ cup (125 mL) ice water

1. Whisk together the flour, sugar and salt in a medium bowl. Using the large holes of a box grater, grate the butter into the flour as quickly as you can. Using your fingers, toss the butter with the flour to coat it, then rub it between your fingers until it resembles cornmeal. It's fine if there are a few lumps of butter.

2. Pour in the water and use your hands to bring the ingredients together into a rough, shaggy mass. Don't overwork it. If necessary, add a little more ice water, a few drops at a time.

3. Turn the pie dough out onto a clean counter and divide it in two. Bring each clump of dough together into a ball and flatten it slightly with your palm. Wrap each disc tightly in plastic wrap and refrigerate for at least 1 hour or up to 3 days. This helps to relax the dough and will yield a flakier pastry.

4. Lightly flour a clean counter and roll one disc into an 11-inch (28 cm) circle. It doesn't have to be precise, but it does need to be a few inches wider than your pie plate. Slide an offset spatula all the way around the pastry to ensure that it is not sticking to the counter.

5. Loosely roll the dough over the rolling pin and transfer the pastry to a 9-inch (23 cm) pie plate. Gently press it into the pan. Trim the edges, leaving a 1-inch (2.5 cm) overhang.

FOR A SINGLE-CRUST PIE: Tuck the overhang under and into the pan; press to seal. Crimp the edges if desired. Refrigerate the pie shell until ready to use. The remaining disc of dough can be frozen for up to 6 months.

FOR A DOUBLE-CRUST PIE: Do not fold the overhang. Proceed according to your recipe.

Preserves Pantry

There's a tall pantry in a corner of my kitchen that holds an ever-rotating stock of foods in jars of all colours, shapes and sizes. It is a collection of everyday staples such as canned whole tomatoes and sandwich pickles, as well as specialty items like pickled Quebec fiddleheads and triple berry jam, all preserved during the peak of their season.

Home canning is no more complicated than home cooking; if you can follow a recipe for soup or a cake, you too can put up produce in the effort to save the best of the season. Initially it may seem daunting, with too many steps to stay on top of, but one recipe is all it takes to usher you into a world where preserving summer becomes second nature.

Canning is a year-round custom in our kitchen. It's yet another project that the whole family gets involved in together. It might be a Saturday morning in August when we all wash and chop vegetables for Summertime Salsa (page 277) or a sunny weekend in October when we pick Cortland apples and bring them home for Slow Cooker Cranberry Apple Butter (page 291).

We first preserve what is local and homegrown, beginning on our homestead with tomatoes, squashes, herbs, rhubarb and more. After that we branch out to deliveries from friends' overflowing gardens. Our neighbour gives us buckets of cucumbers and lets us pick raspberries by the pint in his ever-advancing patch. I turn those beauties into pickles and jam, and the kids skip down the lane to leave a few jars of each on his doorstep as a thank-you. Another friend summons us to harvest crates of Concord grapes from her sunny patio, and these I transform into a no-pectin Concord Grape Jelly (page 289) that the kids go crazy for.

After that, we turn to the many temptations of the market with all its abundance. We stroll among rows of produce stalls with every square inch filled to bursting with the local harvest. I load our baskets with Ontario peaches, Quebec cranberries or an entire sack of fresh corn. I'd love to buy one of everything, but over the years I've learned to discipline myself. I bring home only the ingredients I am certain will yield a preserve that we adore: tiny cucumbers for Baby Dill Pickles (page 270), tree-ripened pears for Spiced Pear Jam with Bourbon (page 286) and crimson cranberries for Cranberry Compote with Port and Pepper (page 282).

It's all hands on deck, literally, as I get us set up in the back yard with a canning station on the stone patio and picnic table. Here in the shade, we escape the heat of the kitchen and benefit from a summer's breeze—and as a bonus, I avoid sticky floors and stove. Taking the work outdoors also seems to feel more relaxed for some reason. I never want our summer canning efforts to feel like a chore, even if we do have a fairly ambitious task list.

"I bet you could eat this entire jar of pickles," I say to my 11-year-old as we funnel hot brine over the jars packed with cucumbers, dill and garlic. "Mom," he says, completely serious, "I could eat five jars." Point made.

When we finish for the day and survey the table laden with our favourite preserves, there is a tremendous sense of satisfaction. I know how much our canned goods will be savoured mid-winter by everyone around the table.

These are those beloved recipes, jars of kitchen staples—jam, pickles and sauces—that keep us fed long after the market stalls are boarded up for winter and the garden has expired for yet another season. It's a collection of both practical and extravagant recipes, because both types of preserves have a place in the pantry. I'll leave it up to you to decide where to start.

7 STEPS FOR CANNING IN A
HOT WATER BATH

Canning in a hot water bath heats food to a temperature that will kill any micro-organisms that may grow in it and also creates a vacuum seal in the jar that preserves the food for up to one year. (For alternatives to hot water canning, see "Saving the Season without Canning" on page 259.) Here are the simple steps that I follow in my kitchen for canning success. Be sure to read through everything carefully before you begin.

It is best to can your fruits and vegetables immediately after you harvest or buy them, for the highest vitamin and nutrient concentration. Avoid using iron, aluminum or copper utensils or pots when preparing your fruits and vegetables, as these metals can cause your produce to discolour.

It's helpful to be well organized before beginning any canning project. Here's what you will need:

⊛ Mason-style canning jars with two-part sealable canning lids called flats and rings. They can all be found at most grocery or hardware stores.
⊛ A magnetized lid wand or tongs for easy removal of lids and rings from the hot water bath.
⊛ Rubberized jar lifters are essential for removing slippery jars from their water bath.
⊛ A wide-mouth funnel for filling jars with preserves.
⊛ A ladle for filling the jars and a saucer for resting the inevitably sticky ladle.
⊛ A very large pot with a lid. It should be deep enough so your jars are covered with about 1 inch (2.5 cm) of water when you place them on the rack.
⊛ A rack for the bottom of the pot, which allows hot water to circulate fully around the jars and protects them from the direct heat of the burners. I use a cake cooling rack that fits my pot.
⊛ Clean tea towels to wipe down jars and lids, and for resting the finished preserves on to cool.

Wash your jars, lid rings and flats in hot soapy water and rinse. Wash any utensils or tools you will be using. Place the rack in a canning pot or a large stock pot and put the required number of jars (without their lids) on top. Fill the pot (and the jars) with water and bring to a boil. Boil for 10 minutes to sterilize the jars. Leave the jars in the hot water to keep them warm and to ensure they don't become contaminated before you seal them.

Place the lid rings on the counter. Put the flat lids in a small pot and cover with an inch (2.5 cm) or so of water. Bring to a simmer and keep warm while you prepare your recipe.

STEP 4. FILL JARS

Once your preserves are ready, use a rubberized jar lifter to remove the hot jars, one at a time, from the hot water bath, tip them to empty out the water, and set them on a tea towel. Use a clean wide-mouth funnel and a ladle to fill the jars. Be sure not to fill the jars completely. Produce expands during the boiling process, so adequate headspace, about ½ inch (1 cm), at the top prevents the jar from leaking or produce expanding and breaking the seal.

Make sure there are no air bubbles along the sides of the jar by tapping the jar gently on the tea towel or by passing a clean wooden chopstick around the contents. Also make sure the produce is submerged in the liquid. Wipe the rims of the jars with a clean cloth and cap with the flat sealing lids and rings. Turn the rings only fingertip tight, meaning tight enough to hold the flat sealing lid in place but not tightened all the way.

STEP 5. PROCESS IN A WATER BATH

Return the filled jars to the canning pot using your jar lifter, and place them so they are not touching each other. Be sure the water covers the top of the canning jars by at least 1 inch (2.5 cm). Return the water to a rolling boil. Start your timer when the first bubbles start, and process for the length of time specified in your recipe.

STEP 6. LET JARS COOL

When your timer goes off, remove your jars from the bath and place them on a heatproof or cloth-covered surface to cool. Let them sit for a day to completely cool before tightening the rings. While cooling, your jar lids will pop, creating a vacuum seal. After they have cooled, press down on the centre of each lid to ensure the jar has sealed completely. Any lids that don't dip down in the middle or that spring back have not sealed. Put them in the refrigerator and enjoy them first.

STEP 7. LABEL AND STORE

Label your jars with the contents and the date. Write directly on the lid with a permanent marker or download and print or purchase specialty labels. Remove the rings, as it is best to store the jars without them. Wipe down the jars with a damp cloth and store your preserves in a dark, dry place until you're ready to enjoy. One year is optimum, and I frequently store mine for up to two.

SAVING THE SEASON WITHOUT CANNING

Preserving the harvest doesn't have to be just about an enormous canning pot and a pantry full of jars. There are plenty of other ways to save the season, such as by freezing, fermenting and drying. Even though I love canning, my freezer holds a colourful assortment of spreads, sauces and vacuum-sealed fruits because freezing is fast and easy. A combination of preserving techniques works well for me.

Here are some of my favourite alternatives to hot water canning. I hope they will inspire a weekend project or two in your kitchen.

FROZEN PESTO

Freeze ¼ cup (60 mL) portions of homemade Basil and Pepita Pesto (page 247) in muffin tins. Once frozen, pop out the pucks and vacuum-seal them for the freezer. Alternatively, freeze in ½-cup (125 mL) jars, leaving ½ inch (1 cm) of headspace.

FROZEN FRUIT

Freeze chopped rhubarb, strawberries, raspberries, blueberries, sliced peaches or cranberries in a single layer on a rimmed baking sheet. Transfer the frozen fruit to resealable plastic freezer bags or seal with a vacuum sealer in a heavy-duty plastic bag. Keep frozen for up to 1 year.

PRESERVED LEMONS

Pack lemons in salt and their own juices for a refrigerator preserve, Preserved Meyer Lemons with Bay Leaf (page 263). They keep for months and only get better with age.

FROZEN ROASTED TOMATOES IN OIL

Prepare steps 1 to 3 of the Slow-Roasted Tomato and Ricotta Tartines (page 105). Pack the slow-roasted tomato slices into wide-mouth half-pint (250 mL) jars and top up with olive oil; add a clove of garlic and a sprig of rosemary to flavour the oil. Cover with a lid and freeze for up to 1 year. The tomatoes reconstitute beautifully for salads, pizza toppings or sandwiches.

HERB COMPOUND BUTTER

Mince a few tablespoons of parsley, dill or sage with a little garlic, then mash it into 1 cup (250 mL) of softened butter. Shape the compound butter into a log, wrap it in plastic wrap and stash in the freezer for up to 6 months. Slice and use for topping steaks, fish or pasta.

HOMEMADE SAUERKRAUT

Ferment heads of young green cabbage for a few jars of Simple Sauerkraut (page 268). Store in the fridge for a few months or freeze for up to 1 year.

PUMPKIN OR SQUASH PURÉE

Roast winter squash and blend into a purée (see page 177). Transfer to half-pint (250 mL) jars and store in the freezer for up to 1 year.

REFRIGERATOR PICKLES

Experiment with refrigerator pickles, because if my kids can, you can too. Start with Baby Dill Pickles (page 270) and then move on to quick pickled carrots and more. Pickles will keep for several months in the refrigerator. I find they are at their peak after 4 weeks.

ROASTED BERRIES

Slow-roast berries on a rimmed baking sheet for a few hours at 275°F (140°C), then transfer them to half-pint (250 mL) jars with their own juices. Top with lids, cool to room temperature, then freeze for up to 1 year. Use for topping pancakes, stirring into yogurt or folding into whipped cream.

DRIED HERBS

Cut and dry fresh garden herbs for future culinary use. Gather about 4 to 6 stems in a bunch and tie with kitchen twine. Hang upside down in a warm dry place until dried, then separate the leaves (discard stems) and transfer to an airtight jar. Use within 1 year.

FROZEN VEGETABLES

Freeze cut-up stir-fry vegetables such as snap peas, broccoli, cauliflower, carrots and sweet peppers by blanching them quickly in boiling water, cooling in an ice bath and draining well. Store in freezer bags and freeze for up to 1 year.

DEHYDRATED STONE FRUIT

Slow-roast pitted halves of peaches, plums or apricots in a 200°F (100°C) oven until chewy, about 12 hours, depending on the fruit. Package in jars or bags and freeze for up to 6 months.

FRESH BERRY VINEGAR

Infuse vinegar with ripe berries for a vibrant summertime vinegar that makes a great base for salads. Try cup-for-cup raspberries and red wine vinegar, strawberries and white balsamic, or blueberries and white wine vinegar. Infuse vinegar in a covered jar for 1 week in a cool dry place, then strain out the fruit. Stored in a sterilized jar, the remaining vinegar will keep for 1 year without refrigeration.

> TIP: *I store food in glass or clear plastic so I can instantly see what is inside. I use canning jars, Weck jars and most any recycled jar from the kitchen. Try to use straight sided jars rather than the jars with shoulders, or you risk cracking the jars.*
>
> *Leave 2 inches (5 cm) of headspace to allow for expansion. Cool overnight in the fridge. Place jars, without their lids, on a flat surface in the freezer. When contents are frozen solid, add lids and label with the date.*

Preserved Meyer Lemons with Bay Leaf

MAKES 2 (1-PINT/500 ML) JARS · REQUIRES TIME FOR PREP

I almost always have a jar of preserved lemons in the refrigerator, especially during the winter months. The tangy, salty citrus rind is a magical ingredient for salads like my Herbed Potato Salad with Preserved Lemons, Olives and Radishes (page 155), pasta dishes, roast chicken, vinaigrettes, marinades and much more. Preserved lemons pair especially well with green vegetables such as Brussels sprouts, asparagus, broccoli and English peas, just for starters. My friend Alana adds them to her homemade hummus, which is a brilliant idea, and supports my theory that everything is better with preserved lemon. I even chop them up and stir them into my Lemon Cornmeal Madeleines (page 92) for a double dose of citrus. Delicious!

You can make this recipe with regular lemons, although I am partial to Meyer lemons, as they are slightly sweeter. Look for organic lemons, as we are using them for their peel.

12 organic Meyer lemons, scrubbed

½ cup (125 mL) kosher salt

2 dried bay leaves

1. Sterilize two 1-pint (500 mL) jars by boiling them for 15 minutes or running them with a load in the dishwasher on the hottest cycle. Place on a clean tea towel and keep the lids nearby.

2. Juice 6 of the softest, squishiest lemons and strain out the seeds. Stir juice and salt together to make a slurry. Quarter the remaining 6 lemons. Flick out any visible seeds, but don't worry if a few remain in the lemons.

3. Pack the clean jars with 3 quartered lemons each. Place a wide-mouth funnel in the jar and divide the salty slurry between the two. It should just cover the lemons. Tuck a bay leaf into each jar.

4. Cover with a sterilized lid and shake well. Open and press the lemons down one more time. To help them stay covered in the salty brine, break a wooden skewer in two and wedge the pieces in the shape of an X inside the jar, just below the neck.

5. Replace the lid and leave the lemons at room temperature for 2 weeks, giving them a gentle shake every few days. After 2 weeks, stash the lemons in the refrigerator for everyday use. It's best to use them within 6 months, but I've kept them for up to 1 year. Don't be alarmed if the liquid gets a little murky; this is normal.

6. To use the lemons in cooking, remove a quarter from the jar with a clean fork. Scrape away and discard the pulpy flesh, leaving only the rind. Rinse it quickly under cool water and pat dry.

Garlicky Sandwich Pickles

MAKES 2 (1-PINT/500 ML) JARS · REQUIRES TIME FOR PREP

❧

The summer sun brings cucumbers ripening by the dozens. As fast as the garden produces, I preserve them in brine for our beloved sandwich pickles. They're a pantry staple year round and an ever-present condiment for summer entertaining. No burger is complete without a slice of dill pickle! I've included directions for both a refrigerator pickle and a canned, shelf-stable pickle.

The grape leaves contain valuable tannin that helps the pickles stay extra crunchy. They are not necessary to the recipe, but if you can gather a few leaves from a friend's vine, by all means do so.

¼ cup (60 mL) pickling salt

6 cups (1.5 L) filtered water

2 fresh dill heads

1 tablespoon (15 mL) yellow mustard seeds

1 tablespoon (15 mL) coriander seeds

1 tablespoon (15 mL) black peppercorns

½ teaspoon (2 mL) celery seeds

2½ pounds (1.125 kg) medium pickling cucumbers, ends trimmed

1½ cups (375 mL) apple cider vinegar

4 cloves garlic, peeled

2 fresh grape leaves, washed

1. In a large bowl, stir pickling salt into the filtered water until dissolved. Add the dill heads, mustard seeds, coriander seeds, peppercorns and celery seeds.

2. Using a mandoline or a sharp chef's knife, slice cucumbers lengthwise 3/16 inch (4 mm) thick. Submerge the sliced cucumbers in the spiced brine and weight them with a saucer or plate so they are completely submerged. Let cucumbers sit in brine at room temperature for 6 to 8 hours.

FOR REFRIGERATOR STORAGE

3. Line each of 2 sterilized 1-pint (500 mL) jars with a fresh grape leaf. Using tongs, divide cucumbers between the jars. Laying the jars on their sides helps to pack in all of the cucumber slices tightly.

4. Measure out 2 cups (500 mL) of the brine and combine it in a pot with the apple cider vinegar. Bring to a boil. Meanwhile, strain the remaining brine, reserving the seeds and aromatics. Divide the seasonings between the jars. Tuck 2 garlic cloves into each jar.

5. Pour the hot brine over the cucumber slices to cover. Cover with lids and let cool to room temperature. Place in the refrigerator and wait at least 1 week before eating. Pickles will keep in the refrigerator for up to 8 weeks.

TO PROCESS FOR SHELF STORAGE

3. First review "7 Steps for Canning in a Hot Water Bath" on page 256 and prepare a hot water bath with two 1-pint (500 mL) jars and lids according to step 3 on page 257.

4. Follow steps 3 and 4 above.

5. Place a wide-mouth funnel in the top of one jar. Using a ladle, fill jar with hot brine, leaving ½ inch (1 cm) of headspace. Seal the jar with a flat and a ring. Repeat with remaining jar.

6. Process jars for 10 minutes in a hot water bath according to steps 5 and 6 on page 258. Cool on a clean tea towel at room temperature for 24 hours, then label with the date and store in a cool, dark place for up to 1 year.

Pickled Fiddleheads

MAKES 2 (HALF-PINT/250 ML) JARS · REQUIRES TIME FOR PREP

❧

Without dispute, pickling is the best way to preserve these seasonal fern heads. Once blanched, they turn a deep green (the same colour as the moss on the forest floor where they first appear) but retain their signature spiral shape. Pickled fiddleheads make a great addition to any cheese or charcuterie board and are a fun conversation starter when skewered as a garnish for my Bloody Caesars (page 166). I also use them as a topping for rich soups and grain or lentil salads.

Look for fiddleheads at your farmers' market in April, right around the time the first rhubarb stalks and morel mushrooms start to appear.

½ pound (225 g) fiddlehead ferns

½ cup (125 mL) rice wine vinegar

½ cup (125 mL) filtered water

1 teaspoon (5 mL) salt

1 teaspoon (5 mL) black peppercorns

1 teaspoon (5 mL) coriander seeds

½ teaspoon (2 mL) cumin seeds

2 cloves garlic

2 slices (¼ inch/5 mm each) fresh ginger

1. Review "7 Steps for Canning in a Hot Water Bath" on page 256 and prepare a hot water bath with 2 half-pint (250 mL) jars and lids according to step 3.

2. Bring a medium pot of salted water to a boil. Wash fiddleheads well and trim the brown ends. Boil fiddleheads for 10 minutes, then drain well and rinse with cold water.

3. In a small pot, combine rice wine vinegar, filtered water and salt; bring to a boil. Reduce heat to low and keep the brine hot.

4. Place the sterilized jars on a clean tea towel. To each jar, add ½ teaspoon (2 mL) peppercorns, ½ teaspoon (2 mL) coriander seeds and ¼ teaspoon (1 mL) cumin seeds. Add a clove of garlic and a slice of ginger to each jar.

5. Pack the cooked fiddleheads into the jars. Place a wide-mouth funnel in the top and, using a ladle, fill jars with hot brine, leaving ½ inch (1 cm) of headspace. Wipe rims with a damp cloth and seal each jar with a flat and a ring.

6. Process jars for 10 minutes in a hot water bath according to steps 5 and 6 on page 258. Cool on a clean tea towel at room temperature for 24 hours, then label with the date. Store in a cool, dark place for up to 1 year.

Simple Sauerkraut

MAKES 1 (1-QUART/1L) JAR · REQUIRES TIME FOR PREP

❧

Sauerkraut is held in high regard in our kitchen, despite its humble standing in the world. It's one fermented food that we always have on hand, for adding to soups and salads, fried eggs and Sauerkraut and Swiss Grilled Cheese Sandwiches (page 87). My Ukrainian grandmother made her own sauerkraut, like generations before her. As a child, I loved a few forkfuls fried up with my perogies—and still do to this day. Of course, my love of sauerkraut goes beyond nostalgia, for it helps to restore the proper balance of bacteria in the gut, and contains enzymes important for digestion.

If you didn't grow up with home-fermented foods, sauerkraut is the best place to start. For one thing, the ingredients are inexpensive. Cabbage, salt and plenty of inactive time are all you need for delicious homemade sauerkraut. The actual *active* time is quite short. Once you have mastered the basic method, try experimenting with flavours by adding a few tablespoons of caraway seeds, lemon zest, juniper berries or black peppercorns.

You can start with a big mason jar, but you may want to eventually invest in a stoneware crock or fermentation jar. I found a crock at a local second-hand store, as well as a wooden kraut pounder. Speaking of pounding, bring the kids in the kitchen and let them help with pounding the cabbage to release the juices—it releases their energy as well!

1 medium head green cabbage (about 2 pounds/900 g)	1 tablespoon plus ¾ teaspoon (24 mL) fine sea salt

1. On a large chopping board, cut the cabbage into quarters and cut out the core. Using a large chef's knife, finely shred the cabbage, cutting it about 1/16 inch (2 mm) thick. Alternatively, shred the cabbage in a food processor with the slicer attachment.

2. In a large bowl, toss together shredded cabbage and salt. Squeeze the cabbage with your hands, working the salt into it, almost as if you were giving it a massage. This helps to break down the cabbage and release its juices.

3. Once the cabbage seems somewhat wet and limp, begin transferring it, a few handfuls at a time, into a clean wide-mouth quart jar or stoneware crock. Pound it into further submission using the end of a French rolling pin (the kind without handles) or a wooden kraut pounder. You'll want to pack it as tightly as you can, eliminating any air bubbles. Continue packing the cabbage into your jar until the cabbage is completely submerged in its own liquid. Find a small plate or lid that fits easily inside the jar and weigh it down with something heavy like a can of beans. It's important to keep the cabbage submerged in the brine.

4. Cover the container loosely with a clean tea towel and place it in a cool, dark place where you won't forget about it. I make room for my crock in my dry-goods pantry; it's out of the way, yet I poke my head in there multiple times a day. Leave the sauerkraut to sit at room temperature for 1 to 2 weeks or even longer, testing it every few days until it is done to your liking. Skim any white scum off the surface with a clean spoon; this is totally normal. A cloudy brine and a bit of bubbling are both good signs, indicating the cabbage is fermenting. However, mushy cabbage or a very unappetizing odour can be clues that your kraut has gone bad. In this case, toss it out and try again.

5. After a few days you should notice the sauerkraut changing in taste from salty to sour, and this is where things get exciting! It's hard to say exactly how long to ferment a kraut, because the time can change with the seasons (it ferments slower in cooler temperatures), the location in your kitchen and variations in the cabbage itself. It can take up to 6 weeks for a good ferment if your sauerkraut is below 65°F (18°C).

6. When you are happy with the tang of your sauerkraut, transfer it to the refrigerator. I transfer mine into a clean 1-quart (1 L) jar and cover it with a lid. Make sure the sauerkraut is covered with brine. Sauerkraut will keep, refrigerated, for up to 3 months or frozen, along with the brine, for up to 1 year.

Baby Dill Pickles

MAKES 2 (1-QUART/1 L) JARS · REQUIRES TIME FOR PREP

When I bring home 10 pounds of mini pickling cucumbers from the market, my children automatically know what comes next. It's their love of homemade dill pickles that spurs me on, and they have come to learn that their assistance is mandatory. They wash and trim the cucumbers while I prepare the spices and the brine, then together we pack them into jars for pickles. There's a science lesson in this kitchen project, and we talk about salt as a preservative, as well as the tannins in the grape leaves that keep the pickles crisp.

Here I'm giving directions for both refrigerator and processed baby dill pickles, as I make both, depending on the day. There's a gallon jar of pickles in my refrigerator all summer long that just gets better by the week, but I also put up a dozen or so quarts of pickles in the fall to last us through the winter.

1¾ cups (425 mL) apple cider vinegar

1¾ cups (425 mL) filtered water

2 tablespoons (30 mL) pickling salt

2 tablespoons (30 mL) raw cane sugar

4 fresh grapes leaves, washed

2½ pounds (1.125 kg) mini pickling cucumbers

6 cloves garlic, peeled

2 large fresh dill heads

2 teaspoons (10 mL) yellow mustard seeds

2 teaspoons (10 mL) black peppercorns

1. In a medium pot over high heat, combine the apple cider vinegar and the filtered water. Sprinkle in the salt and sugar, stirring to dissolve both. Bring to a boil, then reduce heat and keep hot.

2. Line 2 sterilized small-mouth 1-quart (1 L) jars with 2 grape leaves each. Trim the ends from the cucumbers and pack them into the jars. Use a wooden chopstick to manoeuvre the cucumbers into position, packing them as tightly as possible. Drop 3 cloves of garlic into each jar and add a fresh dill head. Measure 1 teaspoon (5 mL) each of mustard seeds and peppercorns into each jar.

3. Bring the brine back up to a rolling boil. Carefully funnel the brine into the jars, dividing it equally between the two, leaving ½ inch (1 cm) of headspace. Seal each jar with a flat and a ring.

FOR REFRIGERATOR STORAGE

4. Allow jars to cool completely on the counter, then transfer to the refrigerator. Leave for 1 week before eating. Pickles will keep in the refrigerator for up to 8 weeks.

4. First review "7 Steps for Canning in a Hot Water Bath" on page 256 and prepare a hot water bath with 2 quart jars and lids according to step 3 on page 257. Place filled jars in the canner and process for 10 minutes according to steps 5 and 6 on page 258. Cool on a clean tea towel at room temperature for 24 hours, then label with the date and store in a cool, dark place for up to 1 year.

Strawberry Rhubarb Chutney

MAKES 6 (HALF-PINT/250 ML) JARS · REQUIRES TIME FOR PREP

I suppose Danny and I began topping everything with chutney when I started muting the heat in the spices of our favourite dishes to accommodate the tastes of three little people around the table—and thus an addiction to this versatile condiment was born. I keep the spices light, but add a generous helping of candied ginger to bring a sweet heat to this fruit chutney. You can serve this chutney with curry dishes like my Mild Chicken and Chickpea Curry (page 205), roast chicken or ham, but my preference is with pork. Heap it on grilled pork tenderloin, glaze it on seared pork chops or serve it alongside a roast pork loin for a perfect pairing.

3 medium onions, chopped

1 pound (450 g) rhubarb, cut into ½-inch (1 cm) pieces (4 cups/1 L)

¾ cup (175 mL) finely chopped candied ginger

1¾ cups (425 mL) apple cider vinegar

1 pound (450 g) strawberries, hulled and halved (3 cups/750 mL)

1¾ cups (425 mL) raw cane sugar

4 teaspoons (20 mL) mustard seeds

1 teaspoon (5 mL) kosher salt

1 teaspoon (5 mL) ground cinnamon

½ teaspoon (2 mL) ground allspice

½ teaspoon (2 mL) freshly ground black pepper

1. Review "7 Steps for Canning in a Hot Water Bath" on page 256 and prepare a hot water bath with 6 half-pint (250 mL) jars and lids according to step 3.

2. Combine onions, rhubarb, ginger and apple cider vinegar in a large, heavy pot. Bring to a simmer over medium-high heat and cook, stirring occasionally, for 10 minutes.

3. Tip in the strawberries, sugar, mustard seeds, salt, cinnamon, allspice and pepper. Stir well, making sure the sugar is dissolved. Reduce heat to medium-low and cook chutney for about 45 minutes, until glossy and the consistency of thin jam. Stir more frequently toward the end so as not to scorch the chutney.

4. Working with one jar at a time, remove jar from hot water and place a wide-mouth funnel in the top. Using a ladle, fill jar with hot chutney, leaving ½ inch (1 cm) of headspace. Wipe rim with a damp cloth and seal the jar with a flat and a ring. Repeat with remaining jars.

5. Process jars for 10 minutes in a hot water bath according to steps 5 and 6 on page 258. Cool on a clean tea towel at room temperature for 24 hours, then label with the recipe and date. Store in a cool, dark place for up to 1 year.

Canned Whole Tomatoes

MAKES 4 (1-QUART/1 L) JARS · REQUIRES TIME FOR PREP

✆

After many summers spent working alongside my mother on mammoth tomato-canning projects, I returned to home canning as an adult on my own terms: no tomatoes. For years I stuck to the more interesting stuff—blushing jams, pretty stone fruit preserves and vibrant salsas—but the first summer I added whole tomatoes to the pantry shelf, my chest swelled with pride. The commonplace canned tomato was more rewarding than I remembered.

Now, a row of quart jars filled with peeled tomatoes suspended in translucent tomato water makes me feel ready for anything—soups, sauces, pasta dishes and much more.

12 pounds (5.4 kg) paste tomatoes, such as Roma or San Marzano

½ cup (125 mL) bottled lemon juice

1. Review "7 Steps for Canning in a Hot Water Bath" on page 256 and prepare a hot water bath with 4 small-mouth 1-quart (1 L) jars and lids according to step 3. Boil a large kettle full of water.

2. Bring a medium pot of water to a boil. Core the tomatoes and cut a shallow X in the bottom with a small serrated knife. Prepare an ice water bath in a large bowl. Working with a few tomatoes at a time, gently lower them into the boiling water for about 30 seconds, then quickly transfer them to the ice water bath. Once the tomatoes are cool enough to handle, slip off the skins with your fingers.

3. Lower the whole tomatoes gently into the jars, using the handle of a wooden spoon to prod them into place. You should fit between 6 and 8 tomatoes into each jar, depending on their size. Continue until all four jars are full. Add 2 tablespoons (30 mL) lemon juice to each jar. Carefully top up each jar with boiling water from the kettle, leaving ½ inch (1 cm) of headspace. Check jars for pockets of air and poke the handle of the spoon down to pop any you find. Wipe the rims with a damp cloth and seal the jars with the flat lids and the rings.

4. Process jars for 45 minutes in a hot water bath according to steps 5 and 6 on page 258. Cool on a clean tea towel at room temperature for 24 hours, then label and store in a cool, dark place for up to 1 year.

TIP: *To safely can tomatoes with the boiling water process, the addition of bottled lemon juice is required, with its controlled acidity, and cannot be safely substituted with freshly squeezed.*

Summertime Salsa

MAKES 4 (1-PINT/500 ML) JARS · REQUIRES TIME FOR PREP

My preferred scooping salsa is a colourful recipe featuring an abundance of summer produce. I can it at the peak of summer, when tomatoes, onions and peppers are cheaper by the dozen. Then we enjoy salsa year round on such things as Slow Cooker Carnitas (page 202) and alongside chips and guacamole.

Whenever possible, I get the whole family helping. Sweet peppers are a great vegetable for kids to practise their knife skills on, because they are not hard or slippery. If I'm on my own, I break up the work by prepping the tomatoes and peppers one day and cooking and canning the salsa the next.

For a hotter salsa, add the maximum amount of jalapeños or mince up a canned chipotle pepper and add it to the pot.

4 pounds (1.8 kg) Roma tomatoes (about 8 cups/2 L peeled)

8 cloves garlic, finely minced

2 cups (500 mL) diced red, yellow or orange bell peppers

2 cups (500 mL) diced green bell peppers

2 cups (500 mL) diced Anaheim peppers

6 medium onions, peeled

8 to 12 jalapeño peppers, halved lengthwise and seeded

1 tablespoon (15 mL) extra-virgin olive oil

2 cups (500 mL) apple cider vinegar

1 can (5.5 ounces/156 mL) tomato paste

1 tablespoon (15 mL) fine sea salt

1 teaspoon (5 mL) freshly ground black pepper

1 teaspoon (5 mL) ground cumin

½ cup (125 mL) fresh coriander, finely chopped

¼ cup (60 mL) loosely packed fresh oregano, finely chopped

1. Bring a medium pot of water to a boil. Core the tomatoes and cut a shallow X in the bottom with a small serrated knife. Prepare an ice water bath in a large bowl. Working with a few tomatoes at a time, gently lower them into the boiling water for about 30 seconds, then quickly transfer them to the ice water bath. Once the tomatoes are cool enough to handle, slip off the skins.

2. Cut tomatoes into 4 wedges and use your thumb to scrape out the seeds. I work over a bowl to catch the seeds and juice. When all the tomatoes have been seeded, strain the tomato water into a jar and reserve it for Bloody Caesars (page 166); discard the seeds.

3. Place half of the tomatoes in a food processor. Blend until smooth, then transfer to a large, heavy pot. (Set aside the food processor.) Dice the remaining tomatoes and add them to the pot. Add the minced garlic and all the diced bell and Anaheim peppers.

(recipe continues)

4. Preheat broiler.

5. Cut onions into 8 wedges, removing the core. On a rimmed baking sheet, toss onions and jalapeños with the olive oil. Spread in an even layer and place under the broiler. Slightly char onions and jalapeños for about 10 minutes, stirring halfway through and keeping a close eye on them so they don't burn. Cool slightly, then transfer the vegetables to the food processor. Process until finely chopped, then add them to the pot with the tomatoes and peppers.

6. Pour in the apple cider vinegar and add the tomato paste, salt, pepper and cumin. Stir everything together with a sturdy wooden spoon. Bring to a boil over medium heat and simmer the salsa, uncovered, for about 1 hour and 45 minutes, stirring every 15 minutes or so. The salsa will cook down and the peppers will soften. Stir in the chopped coriander and oregano. Cook for an additional 15 minutes. Taste and add more salt if necessary.

7. Meanwhile, review "7 Steps for Canning in a Hot Water Bath" on page 256 and prepare a hot water bath with four 1-pint (500 mL) jars and lids according to step 3 on page 257. Working with one jar at a time, remove jar from hot water and place a wide-mouth funnel in the top. Using a ladle, fill jar with hot salsa, leaving ½ inch (1 cm) of headspace. Wipe rim with a damp cloth and then seal the jar with a flat and a ring. Repeat with remaining jars.

8. Process jars for 20 minutes in a hot water bath according to steps 5 and 6 on page 258. Cool on a clean tea towel at room temperature for 24 hours, then label with the date. Store in a cool, dry place for up to 1 year.

Slow Cooker Tomato Ketchup

When you have three children who are as dedicated to hamburgers, oven fries and crispy Baked Buttermilk Chicken Strips (page 81) as mine are, homemade ketchup goes on the "must make" list each autumn. Sometimes I freeze it, other years I'll preserve it in a water bath for the pantry, and every time I get the kids helping to peel tomatoes.

Ketchup is quite easy to make, especially if you employ little helpers for prep and let the slow cooker do the rest. Ketchup is ideal for the slow cooker because cooking it low and slow brings out the depth of flavour in those ripe summer tomatoes. In this recipe I use a little sweet onion and a very ripe pear to enhance the natural sweetness of the tomatoes, as well as to cut down on the amount of sugar.

4 pounds (1.8 kg) paste tomatoes, such as Roma or San Marzano

1 medium sweet onion, chopped

1 ripe pear, peeled, cored and chopped

⅔ cup (150 mL) apple cider vinegar

¼ cup (60 mL) dark muscovado or Demerara sugar

2 tablespoons (30 mL) tomato paste

2 teaspoons (10 mL) fine sea salt

1 cinnamon stick, broken into 3 pieces

½ teaspoon (2 mL) celery seeds

½ teaspoon (2 mL) whole allspice

½ teaspoon (2 mL) whole cloves

½ teaspoon (2 mL) whole peppercorns

1 teaspoon (5 mL) mustard seeds

1 bay leaf

1. Bring a medium pot of water to a boil. Core the tomatoes and cut a shallow X in the bottom with a small serrated knife. Prepare an ice water bath in a large bowl. Working with a few tomatoes at a time, gently lower them into the boiling water for about 30 seconds, then quickly transfer them to the ice water bath. Once the tomatoes are cool enough to handle, slip off the skins.

2. Cut tomatoes lengthwise into quarters and use your thumb to scrape out the seeds. I work over a bowl to catch the seeds and juice. When all the tomatoes have been seeded, strain the tomato water into a jar and reserve it for Bloody Caesars (page 166); discard the seeds.

3. Roughly chop the tomatoes, then transfer to a slow cooker. Add the chopped onion and pear; give it all a stir. Cover with the lid and cook on high for about 1 hour, until the tomatoes have started to break down and the juices are bubbling.

(recipe continues)

4. Transfer the mixture to a blender and purée until smooth. Return to the slow cooker, scraping everything out of the blender. Stir in the apple cider vinegar, sugar, tomato paste and salt. Place remaining spices and the bay leaf on an 8-inch (20 cm) square of cheesecloth and tie into a bundle with kitchen twine. Add spice bag to the slow cooker. Cook on medium, with the lid propped open, for approximately 8 hours, stirring occasionally.

5. Meanwhile, review "7 Steps for Canning in a Hot Water Bath" on page 256 and prepare a hot water bath with 3 half-pint (250 mL) jars and lids according to step 3.

6. Discard the spice bag. Working with one jar at a time, remove jar from hot water and place a wide-mouth funnel in the top. Using a ladle, fill jar with hot ketchup, leaving ½ inch (1 cm) of headspace. Wipe rim with a damp cloth and then seal the jar with a flat and a ring. Repeat with remaining jars.

7. Process jars for 15 minutes in a hot water bath according to steps 5 and 6 on page 258. Cool on a clean tea towel at room temperature for 24 hours. Ketchup will thicken as it cools. Label with the date and store in a cool, dry place for up to 1 year.

Cranberry Compote with Port and Pepper

MAKES 6 (HALF-PINT/250 ML) JARS · REQUIRES TIME FOR PREP

When the local cranberries arrive at the markets like heaping baskets of jewels, I want to preserve every single one. Sure, I freeze bags and bags to add to smoothies and sauces and for my Cranberry-Glazed Turkey Meatloaf with Baked Sweet Potatoes (page 201), but my favourite way to prolong their life is in this compote.

Spiked with tawny port, naturally sweetened and spiced with fresh black pepper, this is a decidedly grown-up cranberry sauce. It comes into its own after a few months on the pantry shelf, once the flavours have had a chance to make friends. You'll want to make a second batch to give away as homemade holiday gifts, as this compote only improves with age.

1½ cups (375 mL) agave syrup

1 cup (250 mL) fresh orange juice

1 cup (250 mL) tawny port

2 pounds (900 g) fresh or frozen cranberries (about 8 cups/2 L)

1 whole star anise

1 teaspoon (5 mL) freshly ground black pepper

½ teaspoon (2 mL) ground cinnamon

2 teaspoons (10 mL) red wine vinegar

1. Review "7 Steps for Canning in a Hot Water Bath" on page 256 and prepare a hot water bath with 6 half-pint (250 mL) jars and lids according to step 3 on page 257.

2. Combine agave, orange juice and port in a large, heavy pot over medium heat. Bring to a boil, stirring to dissolve the syrup. Tumble in the cranberries, then add the star anise, pepper and cinnamon. Bring to a simmer and cook, stirring occasionally, for 5 minutes.

3. Using a potato masher, carefully crush the cranberries. Cook for an additional 7 to 9 minutes, stirring often. The compote will change from a bright red to a deep, wine-coloured red and it will thicken. Remove from heat, remove the star anise and stir in the red wine vinegar.

4. Working with one jar at a time, remove jar from hot water and place a wide-mouth funnel in the top. Using a ladle, fill jar with hot cranberry sauce, leaving ½ inch (1 cm) of headspace. Wipe rim with a damp cloth and then seal the jar with a flat and a ring. Repeat with remaining jars.

5. Process jars for 15 minutes in a hot water bath according to steps 5 and 6 on page 258. Cool on a clean tea towel at room temperature for 24 hours, then label with the recipe and date. Store in a cool, dark place for up to 1 year.

Honey-Sweetened Triple Berry Jam

MAKES 2 (HALF-PINT/250 ML) JARS · REQUIRES TIME FOR PREP

It's funny how this recipe began. It was a last-minute attempt to use up a few handfuls of overripe berries on their last legs. But it ended up as a ridiculously delicious jam that I keep under close guard in my pantry and am very reluctant to part with.

I've kept the recipe small-batch, in case you're in a similar soft-berry situation. It's the ideal jam for thumbprint cookies or for stirring into yogurt, as well as for spreading thickly on hot toast.

Knowing how scrumptious this recipe is, I now seek out "jam berries" at my market—flats of slightly bruised fruit sold at a reduced price. I triple the recipe (which means a longer cooking time) and preserve the jam in a boiling water bath so we can enjoy it all winter long.

½ pound (225 g) strawberries, hulled	½ pound (225 g) raspberries	⅔ cup (150 mL) liquid honey
	½ pound (225 g) blueberries	Juice of ½ lemon

1. Pick over berries and remove any stray stems, leaves or other debris. Wash berries gently in cool water. Drain in a colander.

2. Slice the strawberries and then combine them with the raspberries and blueberries in a medium bowl. Pour the honey and the lemon juice over the berries. Stir gently to coat the berries. Let fruit macerate at room temperature for 3 hours to draw out the juices from the berries, stirring the fruit once or twice.

3. Meanwhile, review "7 Steps for Canning in a Hot Water Bath" on page 256 and prepare a hot water bath with 2 half-pint (250 mL) jars and lids according to step 3 on page 257.

4. Pour the berries and all their juices into a medium, heavy pot. Crush the fruit with a potato masher. Bring to a boil over medium-high heat. Continue to cook for 10 minutes, stirring occasionally. The jam will boil rapidly and begin to thicken as the juices evaporate. Cook for an additional 2 to 4 minutes, until when you draw your spatula across the bottom of the pot, the space stays open for a moment. Remove from heat.

5. Working with one jar at a time, remove jar from hot water and place a wide-mouth funnel in the top. Using a ladle, fill jar with hot jam, leaving ½ inch (1 cm) of headspace. Wipe rim with a damp cloth and then seal the jar with a flat and a ring. Repeat with the remaining jar.

6. Process jars for 10 minutes in a hot water bath according to steps 5 and 6 on page 258. Cool on a clean tea towel at room temperature for 24 hours, then label with the recipe and date. Store in a cool, dark place for up to 1 year.

Spiced Pear Jam with Bourbon

MAKES 5 (HALF-PINT/250 ML) JARS · REQUIRES TIME FOR PREP

One summer I found myself in my kitchen experimenting with pears, my trusty Autumn Spice Blend (page 244) and a bottle of Maker's Mark. The result was a glorious jam worthy of a spot in the preserves pantry. This is the jam you heap onto Spelt Date Scones (page 35)—or eat straight from the jar with a spoon.

I use Bartlett or Anjou pears and recommend using only tree-ripened fruit in the peak of its season. Note that the fruit macerates for an hour with the spices, so build that into your work time.

½ lemon	2¼ cups (550 mL) raw cane sugar	2 tablespoons (30 mL) bourbon
5½ pounds (2.5 kg) very ripe pears	¼ cup (60 mL) bottled lemon juice (see Tip on page 274)	1 tablespoon (15 mL) Autumn Spice Blend (page 244)

1. Fill a large bowl with cool water and squeeze the lemon into it. Peel and quarter the pears, scooping out the core with a small melon baller. Chop pears into ½-inch (1 cm) or smaller pieces and tip them into the bowl of lemon water.

2. Once all the pears are chopped, drain them thoroughly. Return the fruit to the bowl and toss gently with the sugar, bottled lemon juice, bourbon and spice blend. Macerate at room temperature for at least 1 hour (or up to 24 hours, refrigerated) to draw the juices out of the fruit.

3. Meanwhile, review "7 Steps for Canning in a Hot Water Bath" on page 256 and prepare a hot water bath with 5 half-pint (250 mL) jars and lids according to step 3 on page 257.

4. Tip the pears and all their juices into a large, heavy pot. Bring to a boil over medium-high heat, then reduce heat to medium and cook, stirring occasionally, for about 20 minutes, or until the jam begins to turn a golden brown. If you have a candy thermometer, check that the jam reaches 217°F (103°C). If not, watch for it to thicken like porridge, and when you draw your spatula across the bottom of the pot, the space stays open for a moment. Remove from heat.

5. Working with one jar at a time, remove jar from hot water and place a wide-mouth funnel in the top. Using a ladle, fill jar with hot jam, leaving ½ inch (1 cm) of headspace. Wipe rim with a damp cloth and then seal the jar with a flat and a ring. Repeat with remaining jars.

6. Process jars for 10 minutes in a boiling water bath according to steps 5 and 6 on page 258. Cool on a clean tea towel at room temperature for 24 hours, then label with the recipe and date. Store in a cool, dark place for up to 1 year.

Concord Grape Jelly

MAKES 4 (HALF-PINT/250 ML) JARS · REQUIRES TIME FOR PREP

My love of homemade grape jelly matches my children's affection for the spread. Thus we make it every summer, thanks to an abundance of Concord grapes from our neighbour. They arrive by the boxful, in gorgeous deep purple-blue clusters, and everyone pitches in to stem them. Although this jelly is a bit of work, the reward is rows and rows of deep purple preserve that is the perfect pairing to a peanut butter sandwich.

Grapes naturally contain pectin, as does the green apple, so there is no need to add commercially produced pectin. The riper the grapes, the less pectin they contain, though, so search out young, fresh grapes.

Note that the juice strains overnight, so plan accordingly. Lastly, should you ever find yourself with too many grapes and too little time, wash, stem and freeze the grapes to make jelly at a later date.

6 pounds (2.7 kg) Concord grapes, stemmed (about 12 cups/2.8 L)

1½ tart green apples, such as Russet or Granny Smith, washed

2 tablespoons (30 mL) freshly squeezed lemon juice

2 cups (500 mL) raw cane sugar

1. Place the grapes in a large pot and crush them with a potato masher. Roughly chop up the apples—skin, core and all—and add them to the pot. Bring to a boil over medium heat. Reduce heat to medium-low and simmer the fruit, stirring occasionally, for 20 minutes, or until it is a bubbling pot of deep, dark purple.

2. Line a large sieve with damp cheesecloth or a jelly bag and place it over a large pitcher. Carefully pour the cooked grapes and all the juice into the cheesecloth. Strain for at least an hour.

3. Gently gather up the corners of the cheesecloth and tie in a knot. Slip a wooden spoon under the knot. Remove the sieve and rest the wooden spoon across the top of the pitcher. Hang for at least 4 hours. If the juice reaches the bottom of the cheesecloth, pour some off into a large, clean jar. Resist the temptation to squeeze the bag, or your jelly will be cloudy.

(recipe continues)

4. Discard the grape solids but keep the cheesecloth (see Tip). Pour all the grape juice into the jar and refrigerate overnight, giving the tartaric acid crystals a chance to settle to the bottom. (You don't want to include them in your jelly, as they will prevent a good set.)

5. The next day, line a sieve with damp cheesecloth or a jelly bag and place it over a 4-cup (1 L) measuring cup. Carefully pour the grape juice into the sieve, leaving the chalky substance at the bottom—the tartaric acid crystals—behind. You should have 3½ to 4 cups (875 mL to 1 L) of juice. If you don't have quite enough juice, add a little water to bring it up to 3½ cups (875 mL).

6. Review "7 Steps for Canning in a Hot Water Bath" on page 256 and prepare a hot water bath with 4 half-pint (250 mL) jars and lids according to step 3 on page 257. Place two small saucers in the freezer.

7. In a large, heavy pot, stir together the grape juice, lemon juice and cane sugar. Bring to a boil over medium-high heat. Boil rapidly for 8 minutes, then begin the cold-saucer jelly test. Pour a spoonful of hot grape syrup onto a cold saucer and place it in the freezer for 1 minute. When the syrup is ready for canning, the jelly on the saucer will form a thin skin that wrinkles when you push your finger through it. Boil syrup for another minute or two, until the saucer test shows a jelly that wrinkles. When it does, immediately remove from heat.

8. Working with one jar at a time, remove jar from hot water and place a wide-mouth funnel in the top. Using a ladle, fill jar with hot syrup, leaving ½ inch (1 cm) of headspace. Wipe rim with a damp cloth and then seal the jar with a flat and a ring. Repeat with remaining jars.

9. Process jars for 10 minutes in a boiling water bath according to steps 5 and 6 on page 258. Cool on a clean tea towel at room temperature for 24 hours, then label with the recipe and date. Store in a cool, dark place for up to 1 year.

TIP: *Don't toss the purple-stained cheesecloth or jelly bag after you've strained your juice. Wash and dry it, then cut it into 4-inch (10 cm) squares to decorate your jelly jars.*

Slow Cooker Cranberry Apple Butter

This is the prettiest fruit butter around, and my children's favourite breakfast spread. Cranberries give a vibrant pink colour to the typically drab brown apple butter, not to mention a boost of vitamin C. It's tangy, but not too much, and has a luscious, velvety texture thanks to a long, slow cook.

If you don't want to bother with the hot water bath, freeze the fruit butter for up to 12 months, or store it for up to 3 weeks in the refrigerator.

6 pounds (2.7 kg) organic Cortland apples (or other sauce apple such as Empire, Fuji, McIntosh or Spartan)

1 pound (450 g) fresh organic cranberries, well washed

1 cup (250 mL) fresh-pressed apple cider (unfiltered raw apple juice)

½ cup (125 mL) pure maple syrup

1 cinnamon stick

1. Wash apples well, then core them and cut into quarters. There's no need to peel them; you will sieve everything later, and the skins add colour and pectin to the butter.

2. Combine apples and cranberries in a large, heavy pot. Don't worry if they fill it to near overflowing; they will cook down in a few minutes. Add apple cider, then partially cover with a lid and place the pot over medium heat.

3. After about 15 minutes, use a sturdy wooden spoon to stir up the softened apples at the bottom and distribute the heat. After 15 more minutes, reduce the heat to medium-low and stir again. Continue to cook over medium-low heat for another 30 minutes, stirring occasionally as the fruit breaks down, and scraping the bottom of the pot to avoid scorching.

4. Remove from heat. Place a fine-mesh sieve or chinois over the bowl of your slow cooker. Working in batches, press all the cooked fruit through the sieve with the back of a ladle. Discard the solids. What you have now is velvety, blush-coloured cranberry applesauce. Stir in the maple syrup and add the cinnamon stick. Partially cover with the lid and cook on low for 8 hours, giving the butter an occasional stir. Once the cranberry apple butter is a nice spreadable consistency (it will thicken more as it cools), it is ready to be preserved.

(recipe continues)

5. Meanwhile, review "7 Steps for Canning in a Hot Water Bath" on page 256 and prepare a hot water bath with 7 half-pint (250 mL) jars and lids according to step 3 on page 257.

6. Discard the cinnamon stick. Working with one jar at a time, remove jar from hot water and place a wide-mouth funnel in the top. Using a ladle, fill jar with hot apple butter, leaving ½ inch (1 cm) of headspace. Wipe rim with a damp cloth and then seal the jar with a flat and a ring. Repeat with remaining jars.

7. Process jars for 20 minutes in a hot water bath according to steps 5 and 6 on page 258. Cool on a clean tea towel at room temperature for 24 hours, then label with the recipe and date. Store in a cool, dark place for up to 1 year.

With Gratitude

A great many people helped me bring this book to life in all sorts of different ways. A heartfelt thank-you goes out to each and every one.

Foremost, to the readers of *Simple Bites*, after all these years.

My editor, Andrea Magyar, and the entire Penguin Random House team.

My literary agent, Stacey Glick, of Dystel, Goderich & Bourret.

My incredible crew of recipe testers: Janice Lawandi, April Calo, Alana Chernila, Yvonne Tremblay, Megan Myers, Jan Scott, Haidi Telles, Joshua Wimbush, Barbara Vorsteher, Kevin Bourque, Melanie Bourque, Angela Yu, Andrea Rodgers, Courtney Champion, Jenny Jack, Breanne Mosher, Jamie Pettett, Stephanie Sauders, Cheri Neufeld, Laurie Leibov, Jared Gurman, Michelle Erb, Brian Samuels and Julia Frey. Thank you all for being willing to try something new and for your helpful feedback.

Laura Hols Wimbush, Haidi Telles, Joshua Wimbush and Terrie Smith, for inspiring me with your cooking and allowing me to adapt your recipes for this book.

Dianne Jacob, for your encouragement, "utterly" keen eyes and expertise!

Elizabeth Leon, for sharing your empanada recipe and your kitchen, too.

Alana Chernila, for the words of encouragement and friendship.

Grandparents Bourque and Smith, for babysitting so I could write.

Sherina Philipupillai, for stepping in so I could slip away and write on Fridays.

The Food Bloggers of Canada community, especially Melissa and Ethan.

My friends, both near and far, for your graciousness when this project took up much of my time.

My enormous extended Montreal family. Thanks for baking pies!

Tim and Angela Chin, for joining me for the sequel.

My immediate family, John, Zoe, Haidi, Josh and Miranda, for their unconditional love.

My darling children, Noah, Mateo and Clara, my small but strong support team.

Lastly, to Danny, with all of my love.

About the Photographers

Tim and Angela Chin are award-winning photographers specializing in lifestyle, documentary and food photography.

"We decided to become foodies in New Orleans. Somewhere between the seventeenth beignet at Café du Monde and the plethora of fresh seafood, it dawned on us that our plan to design our short trip around the food we ate would become a way we were now going to view the world—starting in the city where we live.

"Back in Montreal, we fully embraced the food culture that surrounded us locally. When guests came to visit we didn't ask them, 'What would you like to do?' Instead the question became, 'What are you going to eat?' We became food evangelists for the city, taking pride in our local talent.

"We believe food is memory—it brings us back to a place, a community, a state of being. Sit for a meal prepared by your mom, and it tastes like childhood. Food is also deeply personal and can only be fully experienced first-hand. We can use other mediums to attempt to describe it, but try as we might, we cannot taste for someone else.

"Good photography brings us the closest. Like food, photography is a language that requires no translation. It can broadcast a story, interact with our other senses and call us to action. It can invite us to want. It can question us with answers.

"It can ask us, '*What are you going to eat?*'"

Tim and Angela are based in Montreal, Quebec, where they live with their three spirited children. Their adventures can be followed on their website, tchintchineats.com.

Index